FEARLESS GIRL

PRAISE FOR *FEARLESS GIRL*

"As a journalist for over 50 years, I am not usually awestruck by a 'newsmaker.'

But when I met and interviewed Quin in Bangkok recently, I was convinced she was not just a very 'special' Thai girl, but she was 'extraordinary'- a Thai girl who made it all the way from a rural rice field to Hollywood's Biggest Stage. And it's not just a fairy tale your parents read you at bedtime.

Quin's life story makes every Thai proud. Not only that. Her incredible achievements prove beyond all doubts that no dream, however ambitious and wild, is impossible!"

—Suthichai Yoon, primary anchor of the Thai PBS news show and former CEO of Nation Multimedia Group, founder and Editorial director of *The Nation*

"Quin's inspiring life story is one for the books, literally! FEARLESS GIRL should be required reading for anyone that wants to live boldly and bravely well into their later years. From breaking out of the depths of poverty of her childhood to capturing the world's heart, both on and off the Hollywood stage, Quin embodies what it means to not only defy stereotypes around aging, but to always live life to the fullest, no matter how old you are. Quin overcomes impossible odds with her unwavering determination, meeting adversity and challenges as a blessing and teaching all of us that anything is possible when your faith is stronger than your fears."

—Tiffany Woolf, Silver Screen Studios, Founder & CEO

"When we're young we dream of all the things we hope will unfold in our lives. So, why is it that so few of them happen? Fear of failure, self-doubt, and humiliation hold us back from even trying. Quin Bommelje made overcoming fear her way of life. Even today, she defies ageist beliefs that dreams have an expiration date. If you would like to think of yourself as defiant, bold, and audacious read Quin's story. It will inspire you to rekindle your dreams and truly live life to the fullest."

—Bill Shafer, Executive Vice President, Growing Bolder

"This book reveals what drives Quin and inspires her successes in life. When someone this extraordinary shares her insights, you read it!"

—Michael Chapman, Tony Award winner, Millennium Dancesport Championships organizer and former World Exhibition Champion

FEARLESS GIRL

From Rice Field to Hollywood's Biggest Stage

Quin Poros Bommelje

QUININSPIRE

FEARLESS GIRL © copyright 2023 by Quin Poros Bommelje. All rights reserved. No part of this book may be reproduced in any form whatsoever, by photography or xerography or by any other means, by broadcast or transmission, by translation into any kind of language, nor by recording electronically or otherwise, without permission in writing from the author, except by a reviewer, who may quote brief passages in critical articles or reviews.

ISBN 13 paperback: 979-8-9869684-0-7
ISBN 13 ebook: 979-8-9869684-1-4

Library of Congress Catalog Number: 2022918814

Printed in the United States of America

First Printing: 2023

27 26 25 24 23   5 4 3 2 1

Cover and interior design by jamesmonroedesign.com
Visit: quininspire.com

DEDICATION

To my son, Mark and my grandchildren, Emily,
Mark Jr., and Casey and their children
and grandchildren for many generations to come.
May you always be humble.
And remember ... when things are going good,
work harder!

CONTENTS

Foreword | xi

Introduction | xv

PART 1: PURPOSE | 1

Chapter 1: Rain 3

Chapter 2: Dreams 19

Chapter 3: Going................................. 25

Chapter 4: Love 35

Chapter 5: Kim 45

Chapter 6: America............................... 47

Chapter 7: Courage............................... 55

Chapter 8: Faith................................. 63

Chapter 9: Roots 69

Chapter 10: Grow 77

PART 2: PASSION | 81

Chapter 11: Tennis 83

Chapter 12: Dance................................ 93

Chapter 13: Misha..103

Chapter 14: Orlando Audition 109

Chapter 15: Celebrity Judges........................119

Chapter 16: The Golden Buzzer 137

Chapter 17: Adapt.. 157

Chapter 18: The Live Show............................167

PART 3: POWER | 173

Chapter 19: Forever Young 175

Chapter 20: Going Home...............................181

Chapter 21: Bold Challenges 187

Chapter 22: Sacrifice................................. 199

Chapter 23: Humble and Hungry................... 203

Conclusion | 207

Acknowledgements | 211

What can Quin do for you? | 214

About the Author | 215

FOREWORD

There is a sculpture in New York City that became quite famous when it was installed for International Women's Day in 2017. *Fearless Girl* is the creation of the American sculptor Kristen Visbal. The figure is of a little girl wearing a dress and high-top sneakers, standing with her hands on her hips, chin thrust up and out, hair pulled back in a ponytail, eyes glaring straight ahead. The statue of the defiant little girl was initially placed in front of the iconic *Charging Bull* statue, a few blocks away, but it was eventually moved to its current location on Broad Street, opposite the New York Stock Exchange.

The reaction to the statue was immediate and powerful. It became a symbol of strength and boldness, purity, and authenticity—especially for girls and women. Thousands from around the world continued to gather for a selfie beside the young girl holding her ground.

Today, many who visit *Fearless Girl* see a lasting symbol of strength and an icon of courage. They want their daughters and granddaughters to understand that girls can be represented like men have been for centuries, with the same power and awe. They want them to feel hope and inspiration—to know that they, too, can be defiant, bold, strong, and audacious.

I am blessed to be married to the flesh-and-blood version of *Fearless Girl*. Quin is a woman who humanizes all the things Visbal embodied in the shape of a fierce little girl. Quin is a dynamic force and a real *Fearless Girl* in every sense. The fact that she overcame starvation and disease in the rice paddies of her village in Thailand over seven decades ago would be enough to be the beginning, middle, and end of her inspiring story. But that is not how Quin's life unfolded. She has accomplished so much more, and to know Quin is to understand deeply how she has made the impossible possible.

Those fortunate enough to know Quin gain a true sense of what perseverance and determination mean. She has spent every day of her seventy-five years

FOREWORD

growing, exploring, training, and devouring experience—relentless in her pursuit of living life to the fullest. Quin trains her heart just as much as she trains her body.

God has richly blessed me to be Quin's soulmate for more than five decades. I am awestruck by what she has accomplished and, most importantly, by the extraordinary spirit she has become. Quin inspires me each day and has transformed my life in every way imaginable.

I am so excited for you to learn about the incredible life journey of my "Fearless Girl".

—*Rick Bommelje*

INTRODUCTION

"Two minutes, Quin and Misha! You're up next. Follow me, please!" The *AGT* production assistant led us out of the large holding room where the contestants were watching, in spellbound attention, the live show on big TV screens. After just a few steps outside the open door, we were behind the giant stage. I took my spot on the million-dollar set that was built especially for our routine. Misha went in the opposite direction to take his position. The stage lights were off. I could see only the first row of the audience because of the blazing floodlights, but as I looked out into the massive, five-tiered theater, the spotlights were shining brightly on the four famous and familiar judges—Simon Cowell, Heidi Klum, Mel B, and Howie Mandel.

The cheers and applause from the audience begin to build like a wave as Master of Ceremonies Tyra Banks introduced us. I felt tingling excitement in every ounce of my body. In a few seconds, the first notes of "Maniac" would play, and I would be performing at the world-famous Dolby Theater, with a standing-room-only crowd and 17 million TV viewers. I closed my eyes and inwardly prayed. I felt strangely calm. This was the chance of a lifetime, and we were about to show the world what we could do. I was about to be performing on the world's #1 watched live variety television show, *America's Got Talent*… at the age of 71.

I have been blessed with so many amazing moments—from leaving the impoverished Thai village where I was born in search of a better life, to meeting an American soldier who would become my husband, to championship tennis courts, to competing in and winning World and United States

INTRODUCTION

ballroom dance titles, and performing on Hollywood's biggest stage. I've always made sure to seek the opportunities that life offers me, and I've never stopped. Doing so has given me the greatest blessings every day of my life.

I hope my story will invite you to seek every opportunity that life's stage offers you to find your own purpose, passion, and power.

—*Quin*

PART 1:
PURPOSE

*"Purpose is being very clear about
what really matters."*
—Quin

CHAPTER 1

RAIN

Rain meant food. Rain meant life. And yet I sometimes hated the rain as a child.

The first rainy nights of the summer season were always a gamble. When the weather was dry, we had no idea how our thatched roof was holding up. It was made of rice straw, the material my father had available, and it had to be replaced at least once a year, sometimes every few months, depending on how it degraded. When the rain came, we would learn what condition it was in.

Drip. Drip. Drip.

At night, I would pull my mat over my head to catch the falling rain best as I could, because having rain hit you as you tried to sleep was the worst. The next day, there might be sun to dry out the mats, our clothes, and our bodies—or there might not be. Those were my least favorite days because I would get so cold. Whether it was raining or not, there were always outdoor chores to be done, and being wet *and* chilled was so much worse than just one or the other.

It's not like we could throw things into a clothes dryer or run a hairdryer. We didn't even know what those things were; we had no electricity. If we had any dry wood left, my mother might be able to start a fire on what we generously called a porch (really just an overhang) and drape our sarongs over it to dry while we stood bare—we had no other clothes to change into. I didn't have a shirt at all, in fact. In my early years, my parents didn't have enough full-length sarongs for all of their nine children, so mine just wrapped around my bottom half until I reached puberty. Each of us had only one sarong that we wore every day.

As we got older, though, two of my sisters (Laa and Mai) and my mother became talented weavers. Using cotton that they had picked, they would weave cloth and then either leave it white or use plant leaves to dye it—almost always blue, because we had beautiful blue plants, but sometimes they would wait for red leaves to grow. Then they would take the dyed cloth to a tailor in town to make short-sleeve button-down shirts for us. That's how I got my first shirt as a preteen.

Although we wore the same clothing over and over, I don't remember anyone smelling bad—probably because my father insisted we all go to the pond to wash off every night. We didn't have soap (we didn't even know what that was), but a quick dip in the water was better than nothing, even with fish,

RAIN

ducks, and other creatures swimming around us. We all went to the pond together, the older ones covering up their bodies until they were submerged and the younger ones happily ignorant. We had no towels to dry off afterwards, so we just air-dried as we walked home. None of us knew what a toothbrush or toothpaste was, either, but our father told us to use salt to clean our teeth. "Use your finger like this," he would say, demonstrating how to rub our pointer fingers around our teeth to spread the salt around, then to gargle with the salt water five or six times. And you know what? I never got a cavity.

We didn't own shoes. Neither did our friends. When we had to go to the bathroom, we went barefoot into the woods and buried what we left behind—even in the middle of the night.

We were each allowed to go to school for up to four years, starting at around age five. After that point, parents had to pay for schooling. I loved school—it was the highlight of my days—but I knew there was no use in asking to continue. There wasn't any money, as always. Not one of us kids had more than four years of schooling.

You get used to these things. In my early years, I had no idea that there was any other way to live. In my mind, everyone piled into handmade homes with leaky roofs, everyone ate rice for every meal, and everyone's lives were *hard*. In my village, that was probably true. Thailand is the world's second-biggest exporter of rice, and my village, in the Isan province in the northeast, is known as the "rice bowl of Thailand." Our village was of no interest to tourists; it was very rural and poor, and because there were no roads, it was just about impossible to get to, anyway.

Without any machinery, we would prepare the ground, soak the rice seeds, spread the seeds, transplant seedlings in small bunches, fertilize, harvest, and remove the rice from its husks using our legs and feet every morning. Husking the rice was a time-consuming process that involved several of us kids stepping on a "see-saw" mechanism over and over to pound the rice on the ground. It kept my scrawny legs strong.

We would eat some of the rice right away, and we would store some of it in the hut. Rice can be stored for a long time. That was lucky, because we were at the mercy of the elements and had several years of bad crops. When there was a drought, that meant no

RAIN

food for the whole year. We would have some rice stored from the previous year that we would ration until it ran out, but no vegetables or fruit in a dry year. Like everyone around us, we ate what we grew. In good times, that meant a variety of vegetables and some fruit, including collard greens, onions, squash, watermelon, and lots of hot peppers—a Thai staple. Even toddlers would eat hot peppers; they were introduced slowly as soon as a child could tolerate them. Most of us grew strong taste buds, able to handle anything. It was a source of pride.

As I grew, I realized I had a lowly rank in the family. The older children were the more "valuable" ones. They could handle most of the difficult farm work, while the younger ones had lighter responsibilities. My job was to take care of the animals. We had water buffaloes, and I had to make sure they were fed, had water, and didn't get stolen. They were like pets—I could ride on them, and they obeyed commands well. At night, I would tie them to posts next to the house. They wore bells around their necks, so we could hear if any of them got loose. Sometimes I wondered if the buffalo were more valuable than I was since they helped till the soil to prepare it for planting.

Some years we also had baby ducks and chickens that my father would raise until they were old enough to sell. One of the ponds on our land was their home, and during the day they ate snails and insects and wandered in the field. I had to watch over the ducks and chickens to make sure they didn't meander too far or fly off the farm, which the ducks tried to do from time to time. "Each duck costs money," my father told me. "We need all of them to sell, so don't lose any." I used a long bamboo stick to tap the ducks and usher them back if they started to make a getaway. Unlike the buffalo, though, they didn't always obey, and sometimes I would have to jump into the deep part of the pond and grab them so I could put them in their little bamboo duck house at night. You couldn't herd chicks with a stick, though—they were too fragile.

The baby ducks grew faster than the chicks. When they were mature, city people would come to the farm and buy them, for their eggs and for their meat when they stopped producing. The visitors seemed like important people to me, and they never paid any

RAIN

attention to me or my siblings. Farmers' children didn't matter. A couple of times, my father also tried to raise pigs to sell. But because they were too expensive to buy and raise, they didn't make much profit, and he stopped buying them.

As I got older, I was also expected to babysit my younger brothers, but that was less valuable work than farming. When times were good, sometimes my father would bring home a treat for my older sisters. Once, he brought them golden lockets. They seemed shiny and very precious, and I would stare at them.

"Did you bring something for me?" I asked my father.

He shook his head. "Your sisters are older and work harder. They deserve it. You're young and don't need it yet. You'll get one someday," he explained. And that was that. The presents were a reward for the long hours of labor my sisters put in on the farm, doing jobs I wasn't old enough to do. I didn't resent

my older sisters; they were protective of me, and I loved them very much. But the effect that moment had on me was profound. I felt like those presents were a direct reflection of how much father cared about each of us. And since I never got one…

It's not that my parents were ever mean to us. They weren't. My mother was very introverted and quiet; it was hard to get to know her, and most of the villagers gave up trying. She was a teenager when she married my father, who was about ten years older than she was and much more outgoing, and they started having children right away. They hoped for boys, because they would carry the name forward — but instead they had four girls in a row.

"If we have another girl, I'm throwing her in the garbage," my father said when my mother got pregnant again.

On April 24, 1947, out came number five: me. Good thing he wasn't serious.

Somehow, their luck turned after me, because three of the next four children were boys. But that didn't do them any good at the time; the older girls assumed all the hard labor, while the rest of us were mostly instructed to "stay out of trouble"—a directive I didn't always follow.

There were snakes around, and my father taught us which ones were poisonous and which weren't. I stayed away from the poisonous ones, but my friends and I would catch the other snakes and swing them around over our heads. I got bitten many times, but I

RAIN

knew they had no venom. I would also climb trees and sometimes fall out of them, which one of my sisters remembered with some frustration. "Father swatted me when you broke your arm," she recalled. "I was supposed to be watching you, but you ran away."

"Sorry, sis!"

"He swatted me *hard*. Three times."

In a strange way, that gave me some satisfaction: he didn't want to throw me away after all. Swatting my sister was a funny way of saying "I love you."

When you broke an arm or leg in my village, someone would make you a makeshift sling with bamboo to keep it immobilized and hope for the best. I was one of the lucky ones: my right arm healed just fine after my fall from the tree.

If there had been an orphanage around, I know my parents would have sent us younger ones there—not out of cruelty, but the opposite: because there was so little to go around and too many mouths to feed, and they knew we were suffering. They never apologized for the way we lived, because they didn't see any other way, but I could see the pain they felt whenever we went to bed hungry, or when we were sick and there was nothing they could do to fix us.

For me, that was often. I was a sickly child, often spiking painfully high fevers and passing out while my family placed wet clothes or leaves on me, trying to bring my temperature down. Most of the time I wouldn't recall anything that happened after I fainted; there would just be lost moments where I went blank and then came back. One time, though. I lost consciousness, and my body was seizing while my mind hallucinated. At first, I saw an elephant. In Thailand, elephants are signs of good luck and adorn everything from tables to clothing. But in this dream state, I was running away from the elephant, into a long tunnel. It was dark, with a reddish-pink smoky haze. As soon as I ran inside, I heard a rumbling sound and turned to see what it was. Behind me was a giant boulder, rolling toward me. I ran and ran through this tunnel with the boulder closing in on my heels. *Stop! Stop!*

Sweat dripped down my body and I ran in a blind panic, inches from getting crushed to death. I didn't know if I would have the stamina to keep running, but I ran and screamed all alone until finally, I reached the other side of the tunnel, and the boulder could no longer chase me. *I'm alive*, I thought breathlessly, and relief washed over me.

In movies I would see later, whenever someone had an out-of-body, near-death experience, they would see clouds and heavenly visions. I didn't see that—I don't remember any specific scene at the other end of the tunnel, except that I knew it was beautiful, and it felt like I had entered another world. Was it heaven? I don't know, but it was a joyful place. It was then that I began to rouse from my unconsciousness—seeing villagers around me dousing me with leaves dipped in holy water. Candles were lit around me, but everything looked very foggy and dim, like I

RAIN

was still in a tunnel. I didn't have much energy, but I felt so at peace in that moment. I had outrun death.

What caused the fever could have been just about anything. There were so many ways to become ill in my village. We had no refrigeration, so the only way to store chicken or fish meat was to try preserving it with salt and wrapping it with leaves, then cooking it outdoors over an open fire. We were bitten by bugs that carried diseases; we were living in conditions without running water or soap; we were sleeping right next to our siblings, even when they were sick (no one taught us about how germs were carried); and we were constantly getting cuts that would get infected. Walking barefoot everywhere meant an awful lot of splinters and cuts. I would always wait for the white pus to form around a splinter to make it easier to pop out. One time, though, I stepped on a rusty nail. Today, I know that I should have had a tetanus shot, but at the time, I just rinsed it off in the pond and waited for it to heal. I still have a hole in my foot where the nail used to be.

Lice was also prevalent in the village. Because we lived in such close quarters, if someone in your family got it, you were sure to get it, too. When I got lice, my head was shaved. I didn't mind that. I'd rather have a shaved head than hair full of bugs. When I did have hair, my sister cut it for me with a knife or dull scissors that would hurt me. I hated that, but I had no choice. I wouldn't have long hair until I was a teenager, and the same was true for most of my friends.

FEARLESS GIRL

We had plenty of playmates in the village. Even though there were no toys, we found ways to occupy ourselves. We mostly played house and explored the farm when we weren't busy slinging snakes around. All of us were in the same danger of malnutrition, especially after drought seasons, and not all of my playmates made it to adulthood.

The first time I saw a dead body was my oldest sister's. I wish I could tell you about her, but I was so young that I remember her death more than her life. When someone died in our village, everyone would gather for a three-day, three-night funeral ceremony to send the spirit to rest in peace. People would play cards and games, drink, recite prayers and speeches, and stay awake if they could, and then the body—which by then was rotting and starting to stink—would be burned right out there in the open, over a fire, like roasting a chicken. Every now and then someone would choose to be buried in the village rather than cremated, but that was rare. There was no cemetery nearby.

One monk was qualified to start the fire, on six feet of stacked wood under the body. "Let go peacefully," he would say. "Let go of this life." According to Buddhist beliefs, all beings die and are reborn in a cycle called *samsara* until they reach enlightenment, or nirvana. That's the final escape when you can stop being reborn. But before that point, you can be reborn infinitely. If you live your life well, you'll have a better rebirth.

RAIN

If the fire didn't burn effectively, it meant that the deceased person was not allowing their spirit to leave the earth. Relatives would cry. They would pray for the sun to shine, which meant that the spirit was happy and blessed. They would pray that the spirit would be at peace, so the body would burn quickly and they could take the ashes home.

Children would attend and watch the fire. It's hard to imagine why adults thought it was fine for little ones to watch the people we knew being burned, which always took a long time. The experience led to ongoing nightmares—visions that still haunt me today. *I can't breathe,* I would think as the smoke got thicker and thicker around me. Part of the reason was air quality; part was the heaviness that came with losing a piece of innocence. Sometimes the people who died were elderly; sometimes they were not. In the United States, there's normally an order to this, but in Thailand, it was much more unpredictable. There were too many causes of death—accidents, illness, infection, starvation. If someone had cancer, how would we have known? One girl who used to help me take care of the buffalo had a bad cough. Sometimes she coughed up blood on the ground. Then one day, she was gone and never came back.

Every time I watched a body burn, I had trouble sleeping for weeks afterward, and I worried about who would be next. "Please hold me. I'm scared," I would tell my mother, and I would cling to her or my sisters at night. It seemed that the older girls could handle it better, but maybe they were just keeping their fears quieter.

Without real medicine or proper sterilization techniques, we had our own rituals and remedies to try to ward off death. When we got bad bruises, we had to lie down on top of banana leaves, and someone would start a fire underneath the bruise to improve the circulation. (The banana leaf stalks would get hot, but they would never catch on fire, so they were considered protective.) Once, when I was bitten by a centipede and my hand swelled up like a cartoon, I had to sit next to a huge pot boiling over with herbs and spices and let the villagers steam my arm under a wet cloth to get rid of the poisons.

"You must be careful. You don't want to die, or you will be burned," my mother would warn me. That's how adults talked to children. No sugarcoating. So much of my life was consumed by the thought of *not dying*—keeping that rolling boulder behind me.

What if I'm not really dead, but they think I am? What if I get burned alive?

I loved my family; I was very close with my siblings, and I had some good times with my friends, but mine was not a happy childhood. It was consumed by the anxiety of survival. Even back then, I knew *things shouldn't be this way*. I thought about all those times I'd lost consciousness from fevers, and how it might appear that I was dead. I wasn't so afraid of death itself. I dreaded the burning more than

RAIN

anything.

When someone was cremated, it was important to keep the fire going. Sometimes, though, it would start raining while a body was burning. As we stood there getting soaked, the rain would extinguish the flames, and the body would be lying there on display, horribly disfigured, undisguised by the fire. At least when the fire was blazing, you couldn't see the details of anyone's body or face, which made it less personal. But rain made everything shockingly clear. It would stay that way until the rain had cleared and the body had dried enough to restart the fire. A charred, wet, half-burned person is a sight you don't ever get out of your mind.

Please don't let it rain today, I would pray at every cremation.

Rain was life. Rain was death. I sometimes hated the rain as a child.

CHAPTER 2

DREAMS

Poverty is a place void of dreams.

I never dreamed as a young girl. Not the big kind of dreams that most American kids have—like becoming a doctor, traveling the world, or being a movie star. Dreams are born from opportunity, and where I grew up—in the hopeless poverty of a tiny Thai village with no electricity, no plumbing or running water, and no roadways—there was only survival, not opportunity. Definitely not dreams.

I realized the other day, looking back, that before I knew the word *happiness*, I knew the word *survival*. Before I knew the word *love*, I knew the word *survival*, for that is all we had. We clung to land, rain, rice, and rest as a baby does its mother's breast, clawing for the ability to stay alive. Sometimes to live another day felt impossible. Who had the effort to do more than survive? Who had the energy to dream?

Around the same time that my family and I were desperately enduring another grueling day of tending buffalo, herding chickens, harvesting rice, and watching over a flock of children, a young Black man living halfway around the world published a poem he called *Harlem*. Of course, I didn't have any concept of America back then, let alone of Langston Hughes. I was four years old when Hughes published *Montage of a Dream Deferred* in 1951; but today, as my life spreads out in front of me like a wide sarong, it seems that maybe he could have been whispering in my ear from very far away...

> "What happens, Quin, to a dream deferred?" his melodic voice asks. "Does it dry up like a raisin in the sun? Or fester like a sore – and then run?"

I can feel each possibility viscerally. But my dreams as a young girl simply did not exist— until one steamy afternoon, that is, when I was about ten or eleven years old. My father came home from his routine travels to neighboring villages holding a small, strange device. He called it a radio and instructed his children and our mother to gather round while he placed it on our small wooden table. While I watched, wide-eyed and curious, he fidgeted with the plastic dial, as the red indicator matched each of his careful movements. Slowly, painstakingly, my father pushed up on the power switch. As the portable transistor came alive with sound, my future cracked wide open. My world grew exponentially in size that night, as if the straw walls of our tiny hut

DREAMS

had blown away. I was captivated.

Each day, my weary family eagerly anticipated dusk, when my father would enter our hut, let out a long sigh, and shuffle toward the radio. Each night, with the flip of the switch, we would be transported to cities and towns across Thailand and the world. We listened reverently as the baritone announcer enthusiastically declared, "THIS is the SIX O'clock NEWS!" Within seconds, we learned about a war being fought in Vietnam, political unrest in our country, and events happening in faraway places that we could not even imagine.

The radio became one of the most valuable possessions my family owned—even more precious than our buffaloes. My father treasured and protected it fiercely. We were expressly forbidden to go near it or use it. Still, while my sisters and I loved hearing the fantastical voices being broadcast from parts unknown each night, we  soon became bored of the monotonous news. Lying next to each other on the dusty floor of the room we shared with our other, less adventurous brothers and sisters, waiting for the blissful reprieve of sleep, my older sister and I would whisper to each other, plotting to sneak a listen to other numbers on the radio when no one else was present. *The Six O'clock News had* given us a taste of the glamorous world outside of our impoverished village, and we wanted more! And, *Wow*, did we find it!

My sister had a friend in the next village who told her about a show on the radio that she listened to every day. Ahhhh, so there *was* more than *The Six O'clock News that* came out of our radio?! Amazing! Each time my sister saw her, the friend shared with her the radio story of the ever-evolving love of a teenage girl and her young suitor. We did not know it then, but the show was a Thai soap opera loosely based on *Romeo and Juliet*.

One sweltering afternoon, when no one else was around, my sisters and I crouched in a shadowed corner of our hut, gently holding the fragile radio in our hands. With the volume as low as possible, we tried furiously to get the red indicator line to tune into a different number on the dial, to hear voices other than the gruff announcer. Finally, we heard distant but clear sounds reaching out to us through the transistor. We sat in awed silence, finally having found the two star-crossed lovers from Bangkok, and we hung on to each passionate word as they tried to save each other from their respective fates.

Bangkok's Romeo and Juliet sounded nothing like the brusque and abrupt *Six O'Clock News* announcer. Their voices were heady and harmonious, expressing their love for each other in lyrical sentences, with a refined softness. My sister and I

DREAMS

were spellbound as we leaned close to the radio to capture every word they said. I had never heard such elegant, precise, and beautiful speech. I was transformed. And so began my dreams, shaped by the far-off voices I heard in the evening news and the sweet promises of star-crossed lovers.

That same night, as sleep eluded me, I tried to envision who my Romeo was and what our fate might be. As I drifted into a restless slumber, from the recesses of a very small imagination grew an image of a petite, dark-haired, and painfully skinny girl who, dressed in tattered clothes and walking barefoot, made her way through the jungle and across a swollen river to reach lands that were still hidden in haze. Though I squeezed my eyes tight and tried to see the city in my mind, we can't see what we don't know. But in the morning, I heard a voice inside my head tell me, "If the big city is where the beautiful sounds exist, then that is where you must be."

CHAPTER 3
GOING

Our radio opened a space in my brain for dreams, and my dreams, though hazy at first, opened a space for my beliefs.

My parents were Buddhists, like most people in Thailand. Buddhism instructs that there are two minds: one that is vicious and one that is kind. My mother encouraged us to use our positive mind all the time. "Do not think the dark thoughts," she would tell us.

She didn't just lecture us about that—she *showed* us how to be kind to ourselves first, before anyone or anything else, by demonstrating tenderness and loving kindness. Although we were not raised with hugs and kisses, like many American children are, my mother was peaceful, gentle, and respectful. And so, even as a very young girl, I listened to the good thoughts and came to believe my own inner voice above others.

Father, too, would always focus on the positive,

despite all the hardships in the village. "Whatever it takes!" he would say in his stern voice. "Don't let anything get in your way." I took this to mean that whatever my goal, I needed to get it done and not think about anything else. That inner voice—like the faraway ones my sisters and I hungrily searched for as we turned the radio dial back and forth—continued to grow stronger, along with my dream of going to the city. But no one in my immediate family had ever left our village, and no one saw me as a good candidate to travel to the big city. I had been very sickly and starved as a young child—my stomach bulging with air, eyes sunk deep in my head from malnutrition, and teeth everywhere in my mouth jutting in wrong directions. My family had even given me the nickname "Teeth." People still thought of me as small in stature, and, like most of the villagers, I barely had enough fabric to cover my body. When others learned I was dreaming about leaving the village, some of them made cruel comments. "Men will steal you if you go to the city!" one of the villagers warned me. "They will sell you." But when those voices grew too loud, I turned their volume down in my head.

By time I was sixteen, my dream of leaving the village had become my sincere belief—I was desperate to leave. *I had to go!* If I stayed, I believed, I would be *nobody*. Unremarkable. Unmemorable. A speck of dust blowing through a painfully poor place where everything seemed to stand still. I believed that by

GOING

going to the city, I could be *somebody*. Remarkable. Memorable. A shooting star.

And so, one day, I approached my cousin Kaseem, who was three years older than me and had been to the city many times to visit her older sister.

"Kaseem, can I go with you?" I asked her breathlessly.

She looked at me blankly, clearly thinking that I was joking. But I begged her, and she saw the determined look in my eyes.

"Okay, girl, but it's not going to be easy. We'll have to find work to eat and find a place to stay when we get there."

"Okay," I said, without hesitation.

The next day, wearing the tattered clothes I had on my back and taking the only other shirt and sarong that I owned in a paper bag, I met Kaseem and took the first step toward my destiny. I had said my goodbyes to my family, the neighbors, and the village before sunrise. I knew that morning that I was going, unafraid, toward a bigger world and that, although I was breaking away from my family, I was not leaving them. We would always be united.

So Kaseem and I made our way through farmland and rice paddies, walking cautiously on the dirt road, without looking back, for about an hour to the nearest town of Chiang Yuen. There, we took some of the money I had made selling vegetables grown on the little plot of land in our village and bought my ticket on a tiny bus traveling to the next-closest city.

FEARLESS GIRL

It took us another hot, dusty hour to arrive at the large bus station in Khon Kaen, where we boarded another sputtering bus to our destination: the big city of Udorn. We arrived there about eight hours after we began our journey. From the bus station, it took us yet another hour to walk to the small bungalow where Kaseem's sister lived.

We were exhausted. Our feet ached, and our bellies grumbled. Dirt covered us from head to toe, but we didn't care; we were eager to eat with family and rest. We knocked gently but urgently on the door and waited. *Hmmmm.* We called her name, but no one came. Sharing a worried glance, we knocked again—a little louder this time. Still nothing. We carefully pulled on the wooden door, calling out louder, but the door stayed tightly locked. We peered into the front window. No lights were on. Clearly, Kaseem's sister was not there. A curious neighbor peeked out of her bungalow next door to tell us that she had gone to Bangkok and wouldn't be back for a few weeks. Weeks?! We could not have known. We did not have telephones back then, and letter writing (and reading) wasn't exactly a normal activity among our mostly illiterate villagers.

With no place to stay, Kaseem and I became still and quiet. I opened my mouth to speak, then remembered not to give the dark thoughts in my head a chance. Instead, I heard father's loud voice in my mind, *"Whatever it takes!"* Anything would be better

GOING

than staying where we were, unprotected. But Kaseem and I absolutely did not want to go to the Buddhist temple, the *Wat*, at night, because that was where dead bodies were taken for cremation. It was a resting place for all who had come (and gone) before us. The Wat was also where ghosts stayed before they passed on to their destination—a place to rest along their journey to enlightenment. Most Thai people believe in ghosts and spirits and, like Kaseem and me, do not want to sleep with ghosts dancing overhead—especially at night, when we believe they come out to be seen. But we had nowhere else to go, so Kaseem and I stepped back out into the night and followed the curious neighbor's directions to the Wat.

Arriving at the temple, we gratefully found a place to lay our heads. Even though we were hungry and terrified of ghosts, our exhaustion brought us the gift of peace. As my surroundings became gauzy with sleep, my last conscious thought was of swirling blues, greens, golds, and purple—the city colors of Udorn, brightly lit up against the night sky. The lights and sounds entranced me in ways I could not yet understand and lingered in my mind as dreams came to life behind my closed eyelids.

Early the next morning, we set out to find work. Picking a busy street with shops and restaurants on it, Kaseem went in one direction, and I went the opposite way. "Do you have work?" was my hopeful question. After hearing "No" over and over, I went into a small restaurant that was owned by a young couple. I asked the wife, and she said, "We do need help, but we can't pay you much." She asked me where I came from. When she learned that I had just arrived from the village, she said, "You can stay here and eat too."

"Yes, I'll take the job. Thank you," I said instantly, with gratitude in my voice. She led me to the kitchen and pointed to a corner. "You can sleep there," she told me. "Here's a mat for you to use." She also gave me a small pillow and blanket. The concrete floor in the kitchen was very cold, and it was difficult to breathe with all the odors from the food. But it was better than living in the village, and I was earning money. I cleaned, cooked, served the customers, and did household chores. Whatever they needed me to do, I did. I knew this situation was temporary and that one day I would find a better job.

GOING

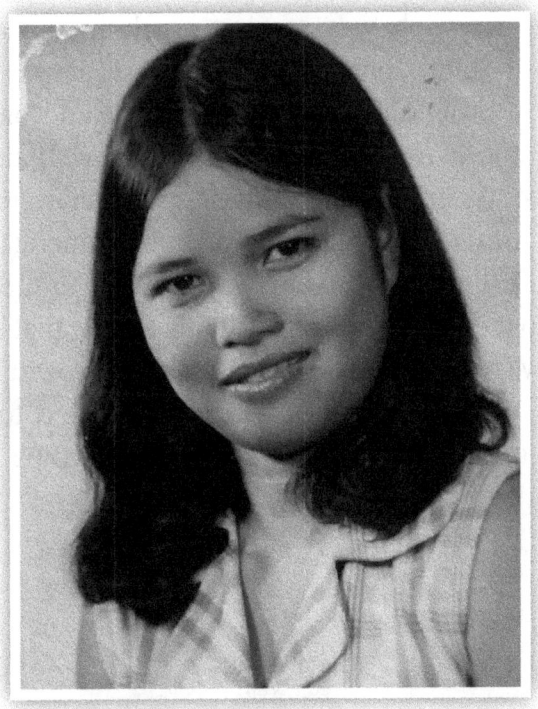

Kaseem and I visited each other every few months. She found a boyfriend who was a Thai soldier, and after two years they got married. They lived right across from the large military air force base in Udorn. The Vietnam War had changed everything in Thailand. The United States had built large military bases throughout the country to help support the troops, creating many jobs for people who lived near the bases. Kaseem told me that her husband knew of a job on the base and they immediately thought of me. She also said that I could come and stay with them. I knew that this opportunity would be much better than where I was, so I left the small restaurant.

FEARLESS GIRL

My new job was serving lunch in one of the outdoor stands on the air force base. It was easier than working at the small restaurant and paid ten times more money. There were many Thais who worked as civilians on the base, and they would buy their meals from stands like ours. American GIs would eat there too. They would speak to me, but I had no idea what they were saying. I knew that education was the only way I could keep growing, so I found a small school down the street and took all kinds of classes, including English and typing.

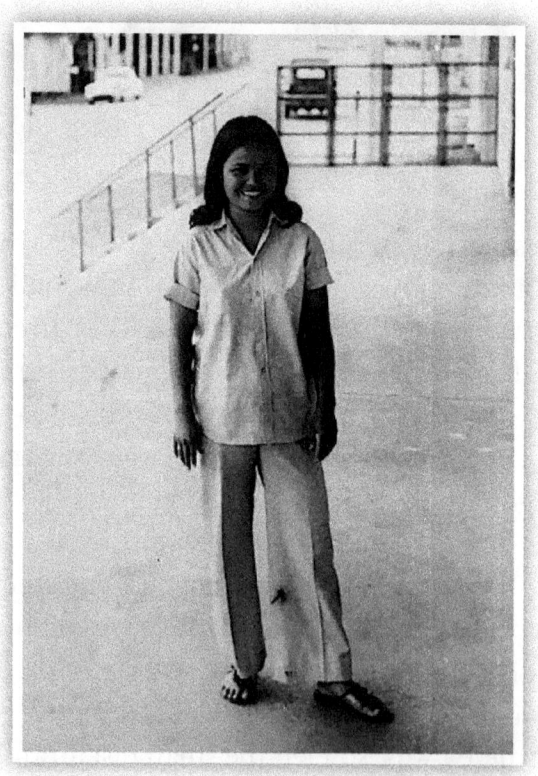

GOING

I loved going back to the village to visit my family. My sisters and brothers were so happy to see me, and I brought them small gifts. They all looked up to me, and I paved the way for one of my older sisters and a younger brother to find the courage to leave home, too.

Dreams are important. But I learned they are meaningless until you take meaningful action. You have to dream it, believe it, do it, and be it to make them come true.

CHAPTER 4

LOVE

While working on the base, I made a lot of new friends. I particularly connected right away with one girl, Nook, who was very smart and had been working on the base for a couple of years.

One day, she invited me to get something to eat with her.

"Where?" I asked.

"Come with me. I think you'll like it." It was a large open-air restaurant off the air base, and Nook said it was very popular.

When we entered, I could see that a mixture of Thais and American GIs from the base were eating there. The atmosphere was lively, and the food was delicious. But when I walked toward the back to the rest room, I heard a loud *Grrrrrrrrrrrr!!!!, and* a big, ferocious dog jumped out at me.

In my mind, I no longer stood in the middle of the restaurant; I was alone in a grassy field on the farm, with only a stick to keep vicious, mean, and hungry wild dogs from attacking my family's buffaloes, pigs, and fragile ducks and chickens. I still had nightmares about wild dogs.

The growling and snarling pulled me back to *this* wild dog. I had no stick to use as a weapon. *Should I run or fight?* The next moment blurred—and then an American soldier rushed forward, caught hold of the dog, and shooed it away. I was safe.

I stepped toward him and said, "Thank you. Thank you."

"No problem," he answered. "That old dog is all bark and no bite. Don't pay any attention to him.

"My name is Rick," he added. "What's yours?"

"I'm Kim."

"That's a nice name. I work at the army Base in Nong Soon," he explained.

"I work at the air force base at Udorn, at one of the stands inside the main gate."

He smiled and said, "Great. I get over there every once in a while. The next time I'm on base, I'll stop by and say hi."

I grinned at him and nodded, then turned and walked back to join Nook. She was smiling at me and asked, "Do you have a new friend?"

"Oh, no!" I said quickly. "A dog jumped at me, and he came out of nowhere and chased it away." Nook had an American boyfriend, and she had a look in her eye that showed that she wanted to talk more about the American GI. I quickly changed the subject, and we left soon afterwards.

LOVE

A couple of weeks later, while I was working, I was startled to hear, "Hi Kim!"

And there he stood—the American GI who came to my rescue in the restaurant. He ordered fried rice and bottled water. "Kim," he asked, "I was wondering if you would be interested in joining me one day for lunch at the army base?"

He seemed so friendly, so I instantly replied, "Yes, I'll come."

"Super," he said. "How about Saturday at noon?"

We agreed that I would take the short bus ride to Nong Soon and meet him there. Rick was waiting for me at the main gate and signed me into the base, which was much smaller than the air force base. Rick said he would take me to the snack bar for lunch. I'd never heard the term "snack bar" before, but I just followed along, very curious. He ordered something he called a *hamburger* for me. When I saw the strange pile of food, I carefully lifted the smooth, fluffy bread from the top and looked underneath it at an unappetizing, dark brown, rounded lump. Red oozed beneath it.

I immediately thought *What the heck is this? Oh my gosh. This is insane. It looks like a little pile of dried buffalo poop.*

I looked up at Rick. "How do I eat this?"

"Just pick it up like this," he said and showed me as he took a big bite out of his hamburger.

Rick waited, smiling encouragement at me. I

lowered my jaw and took a bite of the strange food. Across the table, Rick's smile broadened, but it fell away suddenly as I gagged. My eyes watered as I reached for the napkin. There was no flavor. I was expecting a spicy taste, but there was nothing to it. Just a big glob of tasteless meat.

"Are you okay?" he said.

"I'm so sorry; I can't eat this thing," I said.

"That's okay. How about if we just have some ice cream instead"?

I nodded, and things went much smoother from there. Rick and I talked for what seemed like hours. Even though I didn't speak that much English, I felt very comfortable with him. He gave me a walking tour of the base, and then we headed out the main gate to the bus stop. We said our goodbyes, and he asked if he could visit me the next day. I quickly agreed. I had no idea that this would be the beginning of a lifelong relationship, and that eventually he would become my husband.

For the next several months, we were constantly together, and we both knew we had a very special connection. Rick told me that for him it was love at first sight, while I kept wondering to myself how I could possibly fall for a *farang*—a white-skinned, blue-eyed foreigner.

In addition to many happy moments during the eight months we were together, there were two sad events. One day, one of my brothers surprised me with an unexpected visit. He told me that our father

LOVE

had fallen out of a tree and wasn't able to move. Instantly, I gathered a few things and told Rick that I had to go home. I had already taken him to meet my family in the village a few months earlier, and he said that he would come join me the next day. To ensure that Rick didn't get lost, since he didn't speak Thai, I arranged for the grandson of a friend to escort him to the village.

When I arrived there, father was in serious condition. He had been working on the farm and climbed up a tree to saw off a dead limb. The branch broke, and he fell about ten feet to the ground. No one saw this, and it wasn't until nightfall that a farmer heard his moans and carried him home. The closest clinic was in Chiang Yuen, which was a two-hour walk away. All of my siblings surrounded him and kept speaking to him throughout the entire night, hoping that he would respond. The next morning, Rick arrived, and we arranged for one of the villagers who owned a small pick-up truck to take father to the clinic. We put him into the bed of the truck, and we all piled in. Since the dirt road out of the village was not paved, each bump intensified father's pain. The truck also got stuck several times on the mud road.

When we arrived at the small clinic, the doctor immediately began caring for father and believed he had broken his neck, but here was no X-ray to verify this. We stayed with father the whole day, and he seemed to be resting peacefully. At nightfall, we all walked home—but early the next morning, a villager came running up to our house, shouting for us to return to the clinic immediately. Another villager who owned a truck drove us in. We were shocked to see father on a cot outside the clinic, laboring for air. The doctor told us that he was dying. As we swarmed around the cot crying and saying his name repeatedly, father gasped his last breath. He was gone.

Because of the superstitious fear of transporting a dead person, we couldn't find anyone who would take father's body back to the village in their truck. So, in the rain, my three brothers-in-law and Rick carried father's body, on the cot, all the way back to our farm.

Funerals in Thailand are very important events because they represent rebirth and the passage from

LOVE

one existence to another. Everyone in the village gathered at our home for a three-day, three-night funeral ceremony to send father's spirit to rest in peace. On the fourth day, the monks came to lead the final ceremony. At the end of the ritual, a funeral pyre was built next to our home, and father's body was placed on top. After the monks' chants, all the family

members took long sticks and lit the pyre on fire. We watched father's body disappear into the burning smoke. My "hero" had vanished into the open sky, but he remains in my heart forever.

Months before, when I had brought Rick to meet my family, he had bowed to my father with the *wai*—the traditional Thai greeting—then smiled and proudly announced in his limited Thai, "*Pom loc Kim mak.*" ("I love Kim very much"). Before we said our goodbyes, father took me aside and asked if Rick was going to marry me. I told him that he had asked me. Father looked me in the eyes and said in his loud, confident voice, "Go with him!" His words penetrated my being. Those were the last words he ever spoke to me.

The second sad moment with Rick came a few months later, when it was time for him to return to the United States to be discharged from the army. He told me repeatedly that he would come back for me, but I could not believe him. The reality was that he was just another American serviceman, like so many others, who had promised their Thai girlfriends the very same thing Rick had promised me—only for them to disappear across the ocean. I wanted to believe Rick, and I had a glimmer of hope, but I kept wondering if I was kidding myself.

The dreaded day came, and we had to say goodbye. We both cried hard as we embraced each other for the last time. Finally, he pulled away and said," I'll write to you as soon as I get home, honey!" Then, in a

LOVE

flash, he was gone. The silence was deafening as I watched him run down the street to catch a bus. He didn't look back. My heart was broken in pieces. I felt numb and deeply alone.

Then, two weeks later, John Laughlin, one of Rick's army buddies, came to my tiny apartment, carrying a letter from Rick. I had underestimated his honesty. Maybe Rick wasn't defined by his peers or his Western culture—just like I wasn't defined by my village origins or the suffering of my poverty. Suddenly, the small glimmer of hope I had that I would one day reunite with Rick turned into a spark of faith. Maybe we were meant to be together. Since I couldn't read English well, I took the letter to my school, so that I could understand every word. Rick wrote that his love for me became stronger with each passing day. He told me to be patient and that John would be bringing me more letters. Since there was no phone service, this was the only way we could communicate with each other. My faith grew bigger than my fear as John brought me a new letter each week.

One day, about two months later, John brought me a box from Rick that contained an audio cassette player and a tape. My heart skipped a beat when I heard Rick's voice for the first time since he left. I listened to it over and over again. He said that he could not wait any longer and asked me if I wanted to come to America to marry him—in less than a month. I couldn't believe what I was hearing. Rick

FEARLESS GIRL

said that he had received approval from the U.S. immigration department for me to have something called a fiancé's visa. This meant that when I arrived in the U.S., we would have thirty days to get married. The visa was in the U.S. embassy in Bangkok. I needed to get a Thai passport, and then the embassy would stamp the visa in it.

Was this a dream? Was I going to be with Rick soon?

I traveled back to the village to tell my family. They were all in shock. I told them that I had to go to Bangkok right away to get the visa at the U.S. embassy. I had never been to the capital city before, and all I knew about Bangkok was that it was huge. Prapai, one of my older sisters, had worked in a factory on the outskirts of Bangkok for two years, and she told me that she would take me there. The next day, we took the eight-hour bus trip. When we arrived at the bus station in Bangkok, we got a taxi. Many of the drivers came from our northeast province and spoke the Isan dialect, which made it easy to tell them where we needed to go. I had never seen so many cars, trucks, and people. When we arrived at the embassy, the guard at the gate pointed us to the visa processing center—where I was about to experience the biggest surprise of my life.

CHAPTER 5

KIM

Ralph Ellison, an American author, wrote that our name is the gift of others, but "must be made our own."

For more than twenty years, I was Kim; I was called Kim; I thought of myself as Kim; I told people I met that I was Kim; my brothers and sisters called out to me in the fields, *"Kim! Kim! Come! Come look at this, Kim!"*

Except I wasn't.

After I was born, my father had walked to the Chiang Yuen government building to record my birth. All dates of births and deaths were kept there. He announced my name: "Kim Poros," he declared. But, for some reason, the record keeper heard *Quin Poros*. Even though that name had never even existed in Thailand, *that* was the name inscribed as my legal name seventy-five years ago.

My father never knew. But I discovered it twenty-four years after my birth, when my older sister, Prapai, escorted me to the U.S. embassy in Bangkok to receive my visa to travel to America.

"Your name is not Kim," the official at the Bangkok embassy told me after locating my paperwork.

"Of course, it's Kim," Prapai argued. "She's been Kim all her life."

"No," she corrected us, "look here. It is written Q.U.I.N. not K.I.M. See?" she said, pointing to the individual Thai letters that made up my name.

It was true. All the legal paperwork showed that my name was not Kim but this very unusual, not-at-all-Thai *Quin*.

My name is Quin, I thought, rolling the new name around in my head. It was so strange. Hard. Unfamiliar. But that faraway voice I'd been hearing since I was a very young girl, barefoot and hungry, said to me now: *Whatever it takes!*

I would become someone new. I would become *Quin*.

I was ready to face the unknown in America with my own American.

New Country. New life. New name.

Quin.

CHAPTER 6
AMERICA

The embassy official told me that Rick had arranged for my plane ticket and that I should pick it up at the airport at the Trans World Airlines (TWA) office the day before the flight on March 31—only five days away.

My sister and I went directly to the bus station to return to our village, where we shared the news with the whole family. I could tell that they doubted that I was really going to America, until my sister recounted our visit to the embassy and I showed them my passport with the U.S. visa. My sisters and brothers were so excited for me.

On March 30, the day before I was supposed to leave, Prapai and I got up early for the long trip back to Bangkok. I said my goodbyes to my family, not knowing when I would see them again. When we arrived at the bus station in Bangkok, we took a taxi to the airport. The driver knew where to let us off and pointed to the entrance of the airline offices. We were able to find the TWA office, and my ticket was waiting for me. The agent said that I needed to be back at the airport for check-in at 3:00 am the next morning for the 6:30 am flight. Prapai and I got a room at a hotel close by, and I was so glad she was with me. We stayed up all night talking until it was time to leave for the airport.

The big day had finally arrived, and I had no idea what to expect. Prapai held my hand as we entered the airport, and I checked in. Then, suddenly, it seemed, it was time for me leave. I hugged my sister tight, turned, and walked through the Immigration exit door. After the agent checked my passport, visa, and ticket, he pointed the way to a hallway that led to my gate. As I walked down the long corridor, my father's words popped in my mind—*Whatever it*

AMERICA

takes! I felt ready to face the unknown.

I don't even recall getting on the plane for the first time. I only remember that the flight attendant walked me to my seat. I watched other passengers buckle themselves in, and I did the same. Soon, the plane took off, and I was on my way. I stayed in my seat for hours and hours. Every now and then, the flight attendant would bring drinks and food, but I politely declined, thinking that I had to pay for it. I could see that some passengers were walking toward the front of the plane. I wondered where they were going.

The person in the seat next to mine was a lady with a kind face. I sensed that she wanted to talk with me, but I hesitated because of my English. Suddenly she said, "Honey, would you like to go to the bathroom?"

"You mean there is a bathroom on the plane?" I asked. I had been holding my bladder for hours, thinking that I had to wait for the plane to stop.

"Come with me, sweetie," she said, leading me to the front of the plane and opening the lavatory door. Relief!

Soon, the pilot announced that the plane was starting to descend and we'd be landing shortly. This was the moment I had been endlessly waiting for. It was bright and sunny as I looked out the window, while the plane taxied to a stop.

"Are you getting off here?" the lady next to me asked.

"Yes, I have come all the way to America to be with my fiancé," I explained.

"Oh, that's so romantic. He lives here in Hawaii?"

"Hawaii? No, Orlando," I replied with some confusion.

"Orlando?" she asked me in a concerned voice. "Can I see your ticket?"

I gave her my ticket, and she quickly saw that Orlando was my final destination.

"Honey," she said, "you've got a long way to go yet. Let's go find the gate for your next flight." I followed her off the plane, and we cleared through U.S. Immigration and Customs together. She took me to the gate for my plane to Los Angeles and told me that when I arrived in L.A., I would need to take another flight to Orlando. Then she gave me a warm hug and said, "It was so nice to meet you, honey. Welcome to America, and I wish you many, many years of love and happiness with your soon-to-be husband." Then she disappeared into the crowd. She had been so helpful to me, and I didn't even know her name. I felt like I had been touched by an angel. Later, I learned that when Rick bought my ticket, he had made detailed arrangements with the travel agent for the airline to usher me every step of the way through the long trip. When he found out that the airline did not escort me as promised, he was furious.

It had been seventeen long hours since the plane took off from Bangkok. The flight to L.A. took another five hours. At least this time I knew my way around

AMERICA

the plane and could take care of my needs and eat, too. But when the plane landed and I walked into the L.A. airport, I had no idea where to go. I showed the gate agent my ticket, and he pointed me toward the next gate. I kept walking but never found where I was supposed to go. I didn't even remember which gate I arrived from. It dawned on me—*I'm lost. What if I can't find the gate? How can I contact Rick?* But then I realized that I was in the "land of opportunity." *If I'm lost,* I reassured myself, *so be it. At least I'm lost in the biggest country in the world. I will find a way to survive!* I began asking every person who looked like an airline employee where I needed to go, and finally someone walked me to the next gate. It seemed like I had been wandering around, lost, for hours, but I knew that I was now headed in the right direction. It was nighttime when I boarded, and it would be five more hours to Orlando. I hadn't slept in over two days.

Finally, as the plane was in its final approach to Orlando, I looked out the window and saw a very small airport (this was several years before the mega-airport was built). I walked out of the plane door and down the stairs into the night air. It felt hot and humid, just like Thailand.

I frantically looked around, searching for Rick. I saw a small crowd of people waiting by the outside gate—and then, suddenly, I saw him, waving and shouting my name. *Am I dreaming?* I wondered. I had a rush of feelings—relief, love, exhaustion, confusion—all at the same time. Rick ran over, picked me up off my feet, and gave me a long kiss, and then we hugged each other tightly for what seemed like a half hour as we laughed and cried together. He gave me some flowers, then picked up my suitcase and ushered me into his car. My new life in America had begun. My twenty-four years had changed abruptly in less than thirty hours.

One week after my arrival, Rick and I entered the Orlando City Hall. The city clerk hurriedly escorted us to a back room and conducted an unceremonious but legally binding marriage ceremony, uniting Mr.

AMERICA

Richard Bommelje to Miss Quin Poros in wedded union.

"*Our names, being the gift of others, must be made our own.*"

Ten minutes after entering the Orlando courthouse, just a week after I became Quin, I became Mrs. Rick Bommelje.

I knew that she, too, must be made her own.

CHAPTER 7
COURAGE

My courage has been my salvation for as long as I can remember. It is what has lifted me up, pulled me through, and pushed me over the most dangerous, crushing obstacles of my life. Courage was my companion as I walked with naked feet down hot, dusty paths along soggy rice paddies and as I slept on ghostly floors in the Wat. Courage has been my pilot on transatlantic flights, from my first home to my forever home, and then back again. Courage has been mirrored in both the sky-blue eyes of my husband and the tender coffee-colored ones of my son.

I've always had courage. My father was a very courageous man, and I think it is in my blood. Some have called me a daredevil. Despite my small size, I have always wanted to stretch myself beyond the limits. I had courage as a young girl—getting on a bicycle and trying to ride it, even though I had never done it before. I can still feel the pain in my leg when I fell off and the bike's handlebars punctured my leg, leaving a scar I still see today. I had courage fighting young boys in the village who made fun of me. I had courage leaving the village with Kaseem. I had courage working at the small restaurant and sleeping on the kitchen floor, with the pungent smells and roaches. I had courage letting go and falling in love with an American GI. I had courage leaving my country and family to go halfway around the world to marry this young American, never having been on a plane before. Courage has been my loyal dance partner—the yin to my yang for the last seventy-five years.

So it is not easy for me to admit how much my courage was tested when I arrived in America as a young woman. To say that my first year in Florida was a difficult adjustment is a huge understatement. I knew nothing. What little I had learned in Thailand (four years of a rough, so-called formal education, plus whatever I learned later and taught myself through grit and sheer willpower) emptied out of me like air out of a popped balloon. My first months as Mrs. Quin Bommelje left me feeling utterly deflated.

My courage was tested to its limits. I didn't understand the language well or how people spoke to each other, I had no friends or family, and the American food made my body feel sick instead of nourished. I hadn't eaten Thai food in months. I was alone in a place that did not seem to want me. My husband was all I had, but he worked full-time and went to school at night, so the only time we saw each other was,

COURAGE

briefly, on the weekends. Even then, Rick usually spent most of his free time studying. I had made it all the way to the other side of the world, married my sweetheart, and settled into a small apartment in the land of opportunity, the greatest country in the world. And I was miserable, lonely, and homesick. I thought of my sisters and brothers, my mother, still toiling away in the fields. I missed my family and friends. I missed speaking Thai and eating Thai food. I had culture shock. I couldn't call my family because they had no phone. I would mail letters to them, but it took weeks for them to arrive, and sometimes they never did. It often took many months for me to receive a letter back from them.

I was flattened physically and emotionally. I became wafer thin—so scrawny and gray that one hot summer day, as if seeing me for the first time, Rick looked at me with alarm and took me to a doctor, who immediately sent me to the hospital for testing. The cold, institutional setting made me even sadder and gloomier. With wires running from my chest to a machine, with IV pumping fluids into my arm, and with beeps and buzzers keeping me awake all night, I thought of my father's courage. What would he do if he were in my situation? How had he overcome brutal hardships, day after day, just to keep his family alive? With his loud voice and gruff demeanor, even without expressing it in words, he made me believe that I could do anything. What would he do if he were in my situation?

FEARLESS GIRL

I decided right then and there, that night, on that creaky, hard hospital bed, that I would do whatever it took to turn things around. I committed to myself that I would allow courage to guide me for the rest of my days. The next morning, with dozens of negative test results added to my medical records, I asked Rick to check me out of the hospital and take me home. I crossed the threshold to our small garage apartment, filled with a renewed dedication to my new life. Whatever it took, Rick and I promised each other to build a happy life together—one in which we both could thrive. I would not let myself down, no matter what it took. Rick and I had to make it work, and we grew stronger and stronger, together, from then on.

The day after I left the hospital, Rick found an Asian market in the Yellow Pages. We drove over to check it out. Even though it carried nothing from Thailand except rice, I was buoyed by it. And as if by magic, with each bite of sustenance from my homeland, I became more myself. Rick enrolled me in classes at a community college and becoming fluent in English opened a whole new world to me. I had a new name, a new language, and a new life. Over the years, I have treasured the opportunity to learn and study harder than ever. I was deprived of education as a young girl and have been blessed to make up for that in later life. It was education that inspired me to write this book.

One Saturday morning, while Rick and I did our weekly shopping at the Asian market, an

COURAGE

extraordinary thing happened. There, in the dimly lit aisle where the bags of Thai rice were displayed, I bumped into another young Thai girl. Penn was also married to an American, and she came from a small village in the province next to mine. I instantly felt a connection with her. Penn was so warm and encouraging, telling me that there were other Thai girls living in Orlando. She eagerly invited me to meet them as soon as possible. Penn arranged to pick me up the next week, and we went to her friend's house for my first Thai meal in America. Being in a room with women who looked like me, spoke like me, and who understood me boosted my spirits. For the first time since I stepped foot on American soil, I felt anchored to my roots again.

One of the girls told me that she worked for a Japanese restaurant, and it was looking for help. I told her that I was interested, thinking it would be a great way for me to stay active and improve my English. I was hired me on the spot and met the other girls who worked at the restaurant, most of them Japanese. My job was to be a server, and our uniform was the traditional Japanese kimono. The restaurant was open only for dinner. It was a fancy place, and the food was prepared right at the customers' tables. A few weeks into the job, the manager asked if any of us would volunteer to be tableside cooks. "Yes, I can cook," I immediately replied. I was a quick learner because of my previous experience in Thailand, and before I knew it, I was preparing dinners for hungry customers. I felt like I was performing for them as I skillfully prepared steak or shrimp, always remembering who ordered which entrée.

The manager appreciated my strong work ethic. One day, he asked me if I would be interested in helping with a radio ad to promote the restaurant. "I

COURAGE

like the sound of your voice and the way you speak," he explained. The radio producer wanted an authentic-sounding Asian. The ad would be thirty seconds long, and he would give me a script to read. I practiced reading the ad with a tape recorder until it I got it right. I then read the ad at the radio station, and the producer was very satisfied with it. It was going to be aired the next week.

When Rick and I tuned in, we heard my voice saying, "*This is the Japanese Steakhouse on 17-92 and Fairbanks. We are open six days a week from four to eleven pm. If you are hungry for a juicy and tender Kobe steak and plump shrimp, please come and see us. You will love it!*" The ad was beamed out to the listening audience throughout central Florida. After it was over, I looked at Rick and saw that his eyes were watering. Shaking his head, he said, "I am so proud of you, honey. You just went for it and did an incredible job. You sounded like a pro. Your courage is unbelievable."

I've come to realize that doubt and fear are the enemies of courage. Being a new bride in a new country, where everything felt odd and strange, made me doubt myself and my decisions. Admittedly, Rick and I hadn't prepared for my arrival at all. He hadn't thought ahead about how to navigate our first days and months together. And I was so certain that I needed to leave behind the limited opportunities I had in Thailand that I hadn't given any thought to what my life in Florida might be like. Fear started to creep in like a straitjacket during those first months.

I look back with tenderness at the young girl I was, and I'm fascinated by how much courage it took for her to escape her circumstances, how much trust she had in herself to do big things, how deeply devoted she was to create a better life for herself, and how quickly she said "yes" to new opportunities.

After Rick graduated from college with his first degree, he got a better job, and we were able to move into our first home. Our son, Mark, was born soon after we moved in. A few months after Mark's birth, I began preparing to become a U.S. citizen. I enjoyed learning about American history and was proud to receive my citizenship in an emotional ceremony, along with many other immigrants from countries throughout the world. I am proud to be an American.

My courage has blossomed since those bygone days, providing me with opportunities and joy that I never dreamed possible. Courage paved the way for me to earn my own living before I was remotely close to being a fluent speaker of English. Throughout my life, it enabled me to say "yes" when the world around me was screaming "no!"

As I look back at seven and a half decades of a life well lived, I realize that all the good that has happened in my life stems from the positive attitude my parents taught me. Courage has always been my companion and pilot—and what I see in the mirror.

CHAPTER 8

FAITH

Beyond what I was exposed to by my family growing up, Buddhism was not a major part of my life. Likewise, Rick was baptized in the Christian faith when he was born, but he never attended a church. In fact, neither of us had a spiritual grounding, and we didn't talk much about it.

But when our son, Mark, was around ten years old, I felt an urge for him to have a spiritual foundation, since he had never been exposed to anything. When our neighbors invited us to attend a worship service at their church, it seemed like a good opportunity to explore, so we accepted. The pastor's message was inspiring, the music was uplifting, and the people were very warm and welcoming.

We returned the following Sunday and began attending regularly. After a couple of months, Rick and I met with the pastor. I shared my story with him about my Buddhist roots. He was very interested in learning about me and curious to know what prompted us to attend the church. I emphasized how important I felt it was for Mark to have a spiritual foundation.

"Quin, I respect Buddhism and all the religions of the world. This is God's House, not mine. You are always welcome here," he said. We continued to

FAITH

attend, and two years later, I decided that I wanted to be baptized with Mark and become members of the church. It was comforting to me to find a spiritual home, and I began talking (or praying) to God every day. I told Rick about the sense of inner peace I had when I spoke to God. During a very difficult conflict that Rick was having with one of his family members, I prayed that I would have the strength to help him deal with this serious issue, since it negatively affected the entire family. Rick didn't know how to resolve it, but he did notice how calm I was in approaching the situation. I told him that my strength was coming from God. Through my actions, he, too, began seeking a relationship with God.

Becoming a Christian did not mean that I gave up my Buddhist upbringing. Instead, I built on that spiritual foundation. When we return to Thailand to visit family, we always go to the Wat. Even though it's not a church, I find comfort there every time I visit. God is with me no matter where I go.

We have made special friends through the church. One couple in particular, Wini and Frank Hagy, have become like members of our family. When they learned of my story and we shared photos of our visits to Thailand, their hearts went out to the young children in the village. We told them that we had been supporting the village school for quite some time as a way of serving. Wini spent her career as a teacher and immediately asked if, during our next visit, they could contribute, too, as part of God's work. Wini emphasized that this was not for the purpose of converting anyone to the Christian faith. Her instructions were that we present the donation, and simply add that the Hagy's said "Jesus loves you!" We have done this several times, and their generous gifts have helped many young students continue learning at the secondary and university level.

On several occasions, I have received messages from students who received gifts from us years ago. They expressed how grateful they were for the financial help and how they have gone on and used it to

better their lives. It makes me emotional each time I receive one of these messages, because I know, too well, what the support means to a young student who would like to continue their education, but whose family is too poor to even think about it. These gifts have been life changing for many.

My faith is my rock-solid foundation. For the past thirty years, I have relied on God's strength in so many instances when I could not go on alone. God has helped me in every area of my life. Prayer, to me, is about talking with and listening to God. I tell Him what I am feeling and what I need. Many times, I have received even more from God than what I asked for—in the form of unexpected phone calls with opportunities, clear thoughts about what to do with a big problem, and guidance on which direction to take. At other times, I know that I will need to be patient and wait, no matter how long it takes.

I am grateful to God for the life I have. He has richly blessed me in ways that I could not begin to dream about. As I have said many times, "I love this life and can't get enough of it." All the glory goes to God. I am "on call" for Him.

CHAPTER 9

ROOTS

There's a saying attributed to the ancient Greek philosopher Heraclitus: "No person ever steps in the same river twice, for it's not the same river, and they're not the same person." To me, this means, "You can't go back to the river in your village and expect it to be the same."

That is certainly true for me.

I am asked all the time about where my home is. "Is it in Thailand?" people inquire, "or in America?"

Those of us who have been displaced from our homeland or have immigrated to a new home know that the answer is never simple. Which place is home?

I've lived by my father's mantra— *"Grow where you are"*—so I never felt the need to call one place or another "home." I put down roots and flourished in Florida, and America is my home just as much as Thailand is. Of course, by now I've lived in America for more than fifty years, raising my own family here. So, yes, America is my home.

FEARLESS GIRL

But Thailand will always be my first home. It is the place that created and shaped me, where my dreams were fertilized. Without my roots in Thailand, I would not be Quin Poros Bommelje. And so, over the decades, I have traveled back to my first home whenever I could.

Every visit revealed changes in my village, sometimes so slight they were almost undetectable. Others were dramatic and profound—like the cell phone tower that sits next to our home today. We now have a paved road that cuts through the landscape, and cars, motorcycles, and trucks hurry along it from here to there. Down the street, there is a coffee shop and café—not quite Starbucks, but something that was unimaginable when I was a half-naked girl chasing water buffaloes.

Heraclitus was right. You can't go back to the river in your village and expect it to be the same. On my very first visit home, things felt unfamiliar. My village had changed, yes. But, more tangibly, I had changed too. We were both somewhat new to each other. Everywhere I went, I saw ghosts of my past and remnants of the life I left behind—from the big city of Bangkok and the dusty roads leading to my village to the rundown huts, hungry children, and tall shoots sprouting from the rice paddies. Only the smell of the land stayed the same—the murky, heavy, hot air that seeped into my nostrils.

Rick and I would return to Thailand every two to three years. We first brought Mark to meet his grandmother, aunts, uncles, and cousins when he was six years old. We all cherished these special visits. In a way, of course, I never left Thailand, and my spirit has always been there. It is a wonderful place to visit. Thailand is one of the premier tourist areas of the world, and Phuket, where many Westerners like to go, is heaven on earth—one of the most beautiful places I have ever seen. We took our son there once, and I know why everyone loves it so. It's truly a paradise.

But I didn't like feeling like a tourist, staying in hotels. I wanted a place of my own, where I could wake up in the morning and smell the rice fields, knowing that my family was nearby. I needed a place to stay that felt like it belonged to me as much as I belonged to it. So, we decided to buy the land that once belonged to my father and build our own home there, where I grew up, so I could replant my roots. I spent months traveling back and forth between Thailand and Florida to secure my family's land and make sure that it was rightfully and legally mine. I surveyed the land and carefully chose the exact spot to build our house on my father's rice farm. I hired an architect who helped me put my dream on paper—designing each corner, doorway, and window from the vision that danced in my mind. I had designed my home in Florida, so my experience working with architects and contractors prepared me well for building my new home in Thailand. We started construction in 2007.

FEARLESS GIRL

I traveled deep into the jungle with my sisters and brothers to find the perfect teakwood for the balusters and banisters, floorboards, and windowsills in our new home. The jungle was a portal back in time—I knew where to find the precious wood from the deep recesses of my memory. I stood in the middle of the rice field on what once was my father's land, my sandaled feet firmly rooted on the peat, to call my husband back in America and report on our home's progress—detailing for him the methodical process of building a house piece by piece. We relied on the hands of my brothers, sisters, cousins, nephews, and nieces, creating each piece of material from scratch—not just doors and walls, but also concrete and electric poles for hardwiring.

With every nail, I thought about the rickety hut that I once shared with my sisters and brothers and with our parents, whose only job was to keep us all alive. I am proud of where I come from and my humble beginnings. But after almost a year of construction—at the exact spot where I once slept on the floor with the bugs and rain dripping on my head, in a shack held together mostly by luck—stood a two-story, custom-designed home with a concrete tile roof, running water and electricity, twenty-foot-high ceilings in the living space, air conditioning, a gas stove, and a center kitchen island, with upstairs bedrooms and bathrooms.

In honor of the girl I once was and the family I left

ROOTS

behind, we built a forever home—a structure made to withstand harsh conditions and keep its occupants comfortable and content. Mark has come there with us on a few visits, and someday I hoped to bring my grandchildren.

Our decision to build a home on the rice farm where I was born was not frivolous. We didn't build a fancy vacation retreat. I built my home in Thailand in homage to the ghosts living there, both perceived and real, and to provide refuge for them and for those who are still living. I built it to give back to the place and the people—to provide jobs for my family and people in the village. It is noble work to build a home, and that was just as true for my father, more than seven decades ago, as it was for my sisters, brothers, nephews, nieces, and cousins in 2007.

FEARLESS GIRL

My family members have always had to sacrifice to support each other. I come from a generation that is motivated to help others and be examples to future generations of how to live a life fulfilled. I give back to our village schools, to the Wat and the hospital. I've done my best to give what I can and create something beautiful in a space that was once wrought with pain and suffering—to help make the village where I grew up a better place.

Fifty years after I left the hot, dusty place where I was born—where the spirits of my sisters, mother, and father are rooted—I will leave behind so much more than I ever had. We take nothing for granted. We honor our roots, no matter how painful. I am saddened by the recent passing of my oldest sister

ROOTS

and youngest brother, but from the ashes of those who made my life possible, I have created a haven. I am proof that something beautiful can come from a place made fertile by love.

CHAPTER 10

GROW

The *Noina* is a tropical fruit-bearing tree that grows throughout my village. It is much smaller than the mango trees that also grow from the earth there. One of the national fruits of Thailand, it goes by several different names in America—the sugar apple or custard apple tree. It is nothing special to look at. When I was a hungry young girl tending buffalo under the blazing sun, I might walk past the Noina trees without a glance—except that the sweet perfume coming from its leaf, bark, and flowers would stop me in my tracks every time.

One day, as I walked sleepily toward our hut from the fields where our buffalo grazed, I heard a voice deep inside my head:

> *Stop*, it said gently.
> *Be still.*
> *Breathe in the perfume Mother Earth shares with us.*

Though invisible, it is a gift.
Feel the heavy, perfumed air envelope you.
Close your eyes, girl.
Let your breath out slowly.
Breathe in this place.
Smell that?
That is home.

I stopped and noticed the zigzagging branches and twigs of the Noina covered with bright, deep green leaves. On some of the luckier branches grew fragrant, pendulous flowers with curved, fleshy petals. Soon, when Mother Earth wanted to show off her infinite magic, she would turn those perfume-filled flowers into deliciously honeyed fruit—giving us humble villagers the gifts of beauty, delight, and sweet nourishment. My father would watch his restless children look hungrily at the unripened fruit. If I was patient, I knew, the Noina would soon offer me her treasures, making me feel rich.

Today, I savor the candy-like fruit from a lone Noina tree that grows in my front yard in Orlando, Florida. For more than fifty years, I have called America my home, but the syrupy fruit in my hand transports me back to my first home. How far I have come from my village, I think, and, yet, how grounded I am there, still.

My father said, *"Grow where you are."* When I was young, I did not understand that. But today, seeing how my Noina tree has thrived so far from its

GROW

native soil, I do, deeply and completely. She grew from a single seed I planted, and now she stands strong and pregnant with her legacy—offering shade, nourishment, and fragrant air to those who pause to breathe in the perfume around her.

My Noina tree and I have much in common. We both sprouted from small seeds produced from unremarkable places. There was more inside of both of us than the confines of our surroundings. Pushing against cracked earth and enormous odds, my Noina and I naturally understood that to survive—to bear the weight of beauty, to give generously to those we love, to *flourish*—we must put down roots where we are and go deep. Begin at the beginning, and grow from there, over and over again, through drought and monsoon, bitter cold, unyielding heat, pruning, and blossoming.

I planted my Noina in the center of the walkway that leads to my front door, so that every person who comes to my house must approach it, slowly, breathing in the gifts of Mother Earth. You cannot walk to my front door without passing the Noina. She is rooted in my heart and home, then and now.

> *Grow where you are. Reach toward the sun, my father was telling me, and drink up from the roots. Do not disqualify yourself based on your origins, your appearance, others' beliefs. Grow! Flower! Be generous with your gifts! Make the air around you sweeter! Whatever it takes. We are meant to live extraordinarily!*

I am forever rooted to my village, my family, and my Thai culture. And I am rooted here, in my Orlando home—growing, like the Noina, where I am.

PART 2
PASSION

"Passion is the fire that gives me power."

~ Quin

CHAPTER 11
TENNIS

In my early thirties, I picked up a tennis racket for the first time in my life. Paul, a friend from Thailand, was the catalyst for my athletic epiphany.

"Quin," he said to me out of the blue one day, "I'm taking a tennis class at college. Would you like to go out and hit some balls with me?"

"Hit what?" I asked distractedly.

"Hit tennis balls. Back and forth. To each other. Do you have a tennis racket?" he asked.

"No," I said, but he had piqued my curiosity. I had never played sports in my life.

"No problem," Paul said, undeterred. "Let's go to the second-hand sports shop and see what they have."

Once again, as if by magic, a whole new world opened up to me when I set foot in that shop. I had no idea what to expect—and suddenly, I was in a store full of all things athletic. There were sections for swimming gear, baseball equipment, basketball, football, fishing . . . it seemed endless. And because this was Florida, where tennis is ever-present, there, illuminated under glaring fluorescent lights, were thousands of neon-yellow balls, hundreds of guitar-shaped rackets, special socks, terrycloth wristbands, and everything else one might need to "hit some balls."

I used some earnings from my job at the Japanese Steakhouse to buy a used Chrissy Evert wooden racket and a pair of lightly scuffed Keds tennis shoes. Already dressed in shorts and t-shirts, we went directly to the neighborhood tennis court, where—after Paul's quick demonstration of how to hit the ball with the racket—he and I took our positions on opposite sides of the net. Not wanting to scare me off, Paul softly tossed some balls to me over the net, and I completely missed the first dozen, my racquet making a *whiff* sound with each attempt. I furrowed my brow and concentrated on Paul's movements and the small bright sphere coming toward my chin. I bounced on my toes, trying to anticipate the return, and by ball number thirteen, it happened! I made direct contact—the ball drummed against the strings of my well-worn *Chrissy Evert* and whizzed back over the net, startling me with delight.

Paul was equally delighted that he had found a partner, and with astonishing speed, I got the hang of the rally. With each visit to the tennis courts, I improved, and it wasn't long before Paul and I were playing beginner-level games, with novice serves and two-handed backhands. I felt like a giddy schoolgirl when I played tennis. First thing each morning, I

TENNIS

excitedly looked forward to gripping the racket and couldn't wait for Paul's weekly visits. After about two months, I was confident enough to ask Rick to join me in a game or two. A natural athlete all his life, he was amazed by the control I had over the ball and by the consistency of my precision. After a quick warmup, we played a game in earnest. It was like a bomb going off in my brain.

Suddenly I *had* to win. I needed to beat my husband, who didn't even seem to break a sweat. One hour after we began, my instincts took over, and my competitive spirit caught fire. Paul had introduced me to a sport; now Rick awakened an athletic beast.

I began intently watching professional tennis matches on TV and would study for hours how both men and women played the game. After a few more months, I decided it was time for me to take tennis lessons. I found the best local coaches, including former professionals who had played at major tournaments including Wimbledon and the U.S. Open. After each lesson, no matter how rigorous it was, I would practice for hours with Rick before leaving the courts. That way, I figured, I would progress to the next level.

On weekends, when I practiced with Rick, he would patiently feed me balls for hours and hours—watching me improve my forehand, backhand, volley, and serve each week. When I saw a flyer announcing an upcoming local tournament, I knew that I was ready. I boldly signed my name, *Quin Bommelje*, on the entry form.

My first match was against a younger woman who had been playing for several years. When I beat her easily, my confidence soared. During my next match, I played against a ranked player and lost quickly, but I was grateful for the experience and the loss. I saw right away what I needed to do to compete with opponents who were better than me—and I was motivated

TENNIS

to be the best.

I ate, drank, and lived the game. I got better, stronger, and more prepared and soon began playing Florida State-sanctioned tournaments, where all the ranked players competed. Then came the tournament that changed the game of tennis for me—Daytona Beach. It was already scorching hot when I checked in that morning, and I discovered that my first-round match opponent was the third-ranked player in Florida. I knew how extraordinarily she played each point; I had watched her before from the sidelines, and I felt excited for this opportunity. I took a deep breath, furrowed my brow, and bounced on my toes. "The worst I can do," I told myself, "Is lose straight sets, 6-0, 6-0. But I'll learn lessons that I can use to go forward."

By the time the match began, the Florida sun had made the courts steamy. I was practically panting as my opponent handily won the first set, six games to three. I paid close attention to her serve, her returns, and her position. Instead of letting my instincts take over, I decided to be smart. I realized that I needed to be patient and only attack on the right shots. I was learning from her as we rallied.

Like life, tennis is a game of ups and downs—and there is always the possibility of making a comeback when you are behind. In the second set, the ball went back and forth over the net dozens of times for each point. Rick was the lone spectator at the outer court, and he later told me that he counted the ball passing

FEARLESS GIRL

back and forth over the net forty times on just one point. Unexpectedly, I won the second set, six to four. I stood in disbelief moments after my setpoint. I was shocked.

After a short break, we began the third and final set, and as we took our positions on the court for the first game, a thought washed over me that—to this day, forty years later—has served me well.

When things are going good, work harder!

I promised myself that I wouldn't let up, no matter what. I fixed my focus totally on each point and each swing of my racket from that moment on. I played each point like it was match point. Every game was close.

After nearly three hours, I could see that my opponent was exhausted. She took too-frequent rest breaks, while I was unrelenting. The ball went over the net, back and forth, over, and over. I kept telling myself, *Work harder, Quin!*

Suddenly, with me in the lead and the score at four to two, my opponent finally stood stiff and still. She held the ball in one hand and, with her racket, motioned to me to come to the net.

"Congratulations!" she announced breathlessly and reached out to shake my hand.

"What?" I asked, confused, thinking that I must have misunderstood the rules of this tournament.

"I default," she said, "You win." She turned away, walked off the court, picked up her bag, and left.

I watched her leave. She was not injured; she was

TENNIS

worn down. After hours of battling, I had just beaten, by default, the number-three-ranked player in my age division (thirty-five years and up) in the state of Florida. I beat her with her own style of play, and she could not finish the match because I had exhausted her.

Word of the upset spread quickly through Daytona Beach and Florida's tennis world. After many more tournaments and competitive play—and three years after hitting my first tennis ball with my friend Paul, at age thirty-five—I became the number-five-ranked singles player for my age group in Florida. I also played doubles on a lady's team for many years as the number-one player. We competed at the National Championships at the 4.5 level. With my small size, determined spirit, and unyielding play, I was nicknamed "the annoying gnat." Every time I overheard someone refer to me by that name, I would smile and think of my Father saying to me, *"Don't let anybody tell you that you're too small. You can do anything you put your mind to."*

Put my mind to it, I did! I played competitive tennis for almost thirty years, and I attribute much of my success to my mantra: *When things are going good, work harder.*

Tennis became a family affair. When my son, Mark, was ten years old, he began playing the sport competitively. I was his coach, and he progressed quickly though the junior ranks. As we traveled to tournaments most weekends, parents and coaches were impressed with Mark's relentless style of play,

FEARLESS GIRL

Quin Bommelje new coach at Lake Highland, and son, Mark, No.1 player at Trinity.

Quin Bommelje says the only drawback is that she won't see all of Mark's matches.

TENNIS

patterned after mine. Some parents asked me to work with their sons, especially on the mental aspect of the game. Mark went on to become a nationally ranked player, was featured in *Sports Illustrated*, and earned a scholarship to the University of South Carolina.

Meanwhile, I was approached to coach the girls' tennis team at a prestigious prep school. The athletic director could have searched for officially qualified coaches with all the credentials, but he wanted me, knowing about my success on the courts and Mark's tennis achievements. I coached the team for two years and had an amazing time as I worked with these young, vibrant, dedicated players.

FEARLESS GIRL

For nearly ten years, I also taught tennis in our community subdivision's beautiful tennis courts on a lake. My students included young kids, housewives, high schoolers, and professional people, ages six to sixty-five. It was a such a joy to work with them, and I learned so much from my students and their parents. Always teaching means always learning!

For nearly three decades, the game of tennis was an essential part of my life—until I was diagnosed with pre-skin cancer and was told by my doctor to stay out of the sun. Just like that, my tennis days were over. Retiring from the sport I loved so much was heartbreaking for me. I felt lost. The fire in my belly still burned, and I knew that I needed to compete again. Somehow, I thought, I would find a way to bounce back. And, Wow, did I!

CHAPTER 12

DANCE

My dance story began by accident. Rick and I were invited to a wedding, and there was going to be a live band. Soon afterward, I was watching *Dancing with the Stars* on TV one night, and the thought crossed my mind: *If the stars can learn to dance, can I?* Dancing was something I never imagined I could do—in fact, I had a fear of it. I remember hearing Wayne Newton, the legendary entertainer, admit that he was petrified when he was on *Dancing with the Stars*. But I thought the time had come for me to fight my fear. I was sixty years old, and I wanted to see if I could do it.

Rick was game, and when we walked into the Arthur Murray Winter Park Studio to sign up for lessons, the studio manager, Lukasz Rogowski, greeted us warmly. He listened intently as I told him that I was there to prove to myself that I could do something that I never believed I could.

"I can definitely help you, Quin," he assured me, then introduced us to our instructor. Over the next three weeks, Rick and I learned some basic dance steps, and we actually had fun dancing together at the wedding. It sure beat sitting at the table and waving to our friends on the dance floor.

One week after the wedding, Lukasz called me to find out when we were going to come in for the remainder of the lessons we had paid for. I told him that Rick couldn't make it because of his schedule.

"If you would like to come in without Rick," he suggested, "you can dance with one of the instructors by yourself." With that encouragement, I returned to the studio with a bit of excitement. Like my father's old transistor radio, my introduction to ballroom dancing was starting to open unchartered territory to me. I have Lukasz to thank for that. He opened my eyes to the dance world, and over the years, we have formed a special bond. I sincerely love Lukasz for who he is. He knows my personality and has always appreciated my commitment to being the best I could be. I am so thankful for him and the impact he has had on my life. When I walked into his studio, my life changed again, forever.

One afternoon, when I came in for my lesson, I noticed a woman in the studio who was dancing at a level I had never seen before. I asked Lukasz if she was a professional.

"No," he explained, "she's a student training for a competition next week." I had never heard the word "competition" used with dance before, but Lukasz told me that ballroom dance competitions happened

DANCE

every weekend, all over the country. I was shocked. I didn't know that dancing was like a sport. I told Lukasz about my past tennis experience, and he could instantly see that I was a true competitor.

"Quin," he assured me, "you can be a competitive dancer too." The idea excited me. "I want to dance just like that student, and I want you to be my teacher," I declared. Lukasz replied that he didn't have time to manage his studio and train me, but he promised to bring in a top-level instructor for me. "I know you will like him," he said confidently, "but if it doesn't work out, I will find a way to dance with you myself."

And with that, I charged into the world of competitive ballroom dancing. I would dedicate the same energy, commitment, and determination I used on the tennis courts to compete and win on the dance floor.

The next week, Lukasz introduced me to Romney Reyes—a talented professional dancer and highly experienced instructor—to see how compatible we were. Romney is a perfectionist, with a quiet personality, and from the moment I met him, I felt totally comfortable with him. In the beginning, we danced both Smooth and American Rhythm, and I enjoyed how serious and focused he was on helping me improve. Then, after a year of training, when we started competing in Arthur Murray competitions, Romney and I were thrilled to win the Arthur Murray Superama in Las Vegas, in both Smooth and Rhythm Open Gold. Going forward, though, Lukasz told us that we should focus on American Rhythm only, so I began devoting myself totally to this style. As Lukasz coached us, and we got better and better, he told us that it was time to expand to independent competi-

DANCE

tions against the best dancers in the country.

So, in 2010, Romney and I traveled to the World Championships at the Ohio Star Ball, to see how we could do against the best of the best. We decided to dance in three divisions—my age group, the younger age group, and rising stars. It was a marathon of dance, since most divisions had more than thirty-six teams and many competitors. Romney and I danced from 8:00 am until one o'clock the next morning. As we competed in the preliminary rounds for my age group, we surprised ourselves by how we continued to advance in the competition. Many of the dancers had decades of experience—some starting when they were just two or three years old. To our amazement, though, we made it to the final round. Romney and I vowed to each other to do our best and not focus on

where we placed. Making it this far was already an unbelievable accomplishment. I kept thinking about my tennis slogan: *When things are going good, work harder!*

After the finals were over, Romney and I waited for the results. Finally, the announcer called all the competitors to the dance floor. He began with sixth place, and we thought he would call our names. But no—another team was called. Announcements of winners continued until there were only two teams left. Romney and I were speechless. We held each other tight, and the suspense was nearly unbearable as we waited for the master of ceremonies to announce the first-place winner. Finally, he boomed, "And the 2010 Senior Women American Rhythm World Champions are… QUIN BOMMELJE and ROMNEY REYES!!!"

Romney picked me up and twirled me around as the audience in the large ballroom roared. It was beyond belief. It took several days for this huge accomplishment to sink in. Romney and I had been dancing for just two years, and we had won the world championship. We were also finalists in the younger age group and runners up in the Rising Stars division—all on the same day.

DANCE

Bill Shafer, executive vice president of the highly popular Growing Bolder media company, reached out to interview me after learning about our World Championship. It was especially astonishing, he said, that I only started dancing when I was sixty years old. When he and his film team came to the studio to interview Romney, Lukasz, Rick, and me, he asked me what I liked best about the sport.

"Dancing allows me to express all my feelings. It is like oxygen to me," I told him. "I dance to live—I don't live to dance. I have found a new sense of purpose and passion," I said. As Romney added, "Dancing is a total team sport and we both have the desire to reach our fullest potential." And Lukasz noted that "As a competitive athlete, Quin was used to the physical and mental demands required to succeed. Her dedication to excel is extraordinary."

Bill then asked me, 'What's your next bold move, Quin?"

"Bill," I replied, "I love this life and I can't get enough of it. If God has given me the ability to do this, I'm going to do it until I can't get up. I'm sixty-four years old, and I'm ready to dance against the younger age group."

"All I can say, Quin," he exclaimed, "is…those kids better watch out."

From then on, Romney and I continued to train harder than ever. But life is filled with uncertainty. One day, as we were about to begin training, Romney told me that he had some news to share. Due to family matters, he needed to make some big changes in his schedule. He would not be able to continue the same level of training and travel time needed for us to compete at our current level.

I was stunned. In my mind, I was ready to work even harder, not cut back. But I could see that this was a very difficult decision for him to make. I had always admired Romney's kindness and honesty, and I told him that I completely understood his situation. Still, I could not settle for less. The reality sank in—it was time for us to go our separate ways. We finished our dance partnership on top and remain special friends to this day. I treasure our memories together and am blessed and forever grateful to have learned

DANCE

so much from him.

But inside, my heart was broken. I was so used to dancing with Romney. Who would I dance with next? I decided to pause and consider my next move very carefully. I couldn't stop now.

CHAPTER 13
MISHA

I took some time off from dance to think about my vision, target, and passion for dance and consider my next move. I decided to contact a dancer, Misha Vlasov, whom I did not know personally, but I had watched him dance professionally and admired his skill. I told him that I was searching for a dance teacher and gave him a summary of who I was and what I had accomplished. Misha replied that he was interested in meeting with me, but he lived two and a half hours away from me, up in Jacksonville. To train with Romney, I had only needed to drive five minutes from my house. But after talking to Rick about it, we decided to drive up and meet with Misha and his parents, Marina and Vasily, who owned the Arthur Murray South Jacksonville studio.

The meeting went very well, and I thought that our dance partnership could work. But after sharing the news with Lukasz, he warned me, "This is impossible, Quin. You won't last a week. It's too far for you to make the trip every day! Rick will never let you do this."

I was grateful for Lukasz's concern for me, but he didn't understand my burning desire and level of commitment. I believed my instincts. If I wanted something bad enough, I would do whatever it took to get it—even if that meant driving five hours to and from Jacksonville, four days a week, for the next five years. Rick saw how committed I was and gave me his total support, even though I would wear out two new cars to train with Misha. It was so worth every mile and minute. My next dance journey was about to begin, and it would carry me beyond my wildest dreams.

When I had my first session with Misha in 2014, I entered with a beginner's mindset. "Teach me how to dance, Misha," I said. "I'll let you be the judge when we need to compete." Despite everything I had accomplished, I wanted to make a fresh start with my new instructor. After the next few months, when we got to know each other's personality and dancing skills, I asked him whether he thought I was ready to compete.

"Absolutely," he said instantly, and I appreciated his willingness to go for it. We soon competed for the first time in the United States Dance Championship (USDC). I was sixty-seven years old, and we challenged ourselves to compete in the B Open Gold Scholarship division. At the time, there was no Senior division—and unbelievably, we finished in second

MISHA

place. Over the next five years, our results were astounding. We continued to compete successfully in the younger age group and senior divisions throughout the country and won multiple World and United States Championship titles.

Misha is the most unique person I have ever met. He is very humble, highly creative, and extremely talented. He loves to dance and is so passionate about it. He is not just my dance partner; he is my friend and has become part of my family. We have spent so much time together that my husband and I have adopted him like a son. We know each other's personalities inside and out. We have fought with each other, too, but like family members, and we have always come back together again. I love Misha with all my heart.

Our many successes, it turned out, were the preparation for our hardest and boldest challenge yet. Misha and I decided to try out for *America's Got Talent!* What happened next was bigger and wilder than any competition we had ever experienced, or could even imagine.

MISHA

CHAPTER 14

ORLANDO AUDITION

I spent a lifetime cultivating my dreams. I always knew that I wanted to be someone. To be seen. To show the world the beauty that lives inside my body. To matter. And in November 2017, the door to those dreams opened, literally and figuratively.

Misha and I learned that *America's Got Talent* was launching its thirteenth season with open auditions in ten cities. Surprisingly, Orlando was the first stop in the series, and the audition would be held in two months. The timing was perfect. We were coming off an unbelievable year of success, so we completed the multi-page application form and sent it off. A few days later, we got a response confirming our entry, with instructions to be at the Orange County Convention Center on November 5.

Misha and I chose to dance the Swing for the audition, since it was upbeat, fast, and exciting. In addition to being an amazing dancer, Misha is also a fabulous choreographer. He took our dance routine and revamped it, adding tricks, spins, and lifts to make it appealing to a larger audience beyond the ballroom dance world. With my daredevil spirit, I was so excited to see how it was taking shape. Since we would need help with the new lifts and spins, Misha asked Craig Smith—one of the world's best Theater Arts dancers—to coach us. Craig had performed on *America's Got Talent* two years earlier with his professional partner, so he was the perfect person to work with us. For the next two months, we practiced our routine five days a week. The Vlasov's opened a second studio in St. Augustine, which was thirty minutes closer to Orlando, and we alternated our training at the two studios.

On *AGT* Audition Day—a bright, sunny central Florida Sunday morning—Misha, Rick, and I drove to the Orange County Convention Center. We waited in a six-hour line with thousands of other contestants, all of whom had dreams like ours—to show the world the magic contained within us.

There was every kind of act imaginable—comedians, acrobats, singers, ventriloquists, and dance teams, to name just a few. Misha and I were dressed in our custom-designed, glistening ballroom dance costumes, and we enjoyed chatting with the contestants next to us as the line snaked into the huge complex.

ORLANDO AUDITION

We checked in and were given a number. Auditions were running behind, so we could expect another two- to three-hour wait. When our number was finally called, we were part of a group of ten dancers and dance teams. We were all guided into a room with a dance floor and told to take a seat in the back while each act performed. The celebrity judges we see on TV were not involved with preliminary auditions. There was only one judge in the room—an older man who looked very experienced, like he had been doing this for a long time.

After eight teams had performed, the assistant suddenly called our number, and we approached the big X on the dance floor in front of the judge.

"What are your names?" he asked us.

"I'm Quin Bommelje."

"I'm Misha Vlasov."

"And your ages?"

"I'm thirty-five," Misha said, and I followed with "I'm seventy years old."

Instantly, I heard the voices of other performers.

"You've got to be kidding me! You're seventy! Unbelievable!"

With that, the judge said, "You're on!"

And in only ninety seconds—with Misha matching his moves to mine, lifting me, spinning me overhead, and dropping me in death-defying moves—my body became a portal to the fearless spirit living not-so-deep within me. I hit every mark. I allowed my self-assurance to drive my performance—trusting my abilities, my athleticism, my dance partner, and my faith. My whole life had led me to this very moment. Misha and I danced our hearts out.

And after ninety seconds, when our song ended and our bodies froze in the final move, the other contestants burst into applause and cheered. The judge scribbled a few notes and thanked us. As we returned to our seats, the other dancers congratulated us on our performance. After the last act ended, the judge said, "Thank you. You all did great. We will let you know by January if you make it. If you don't

ORLANDO AUDITION

hear from us, that means you didn't make it." The assistant then led us all out of the room.

As we were gathering our belongings outside, she called out, "Misha! Quin! Wait just a second. Come with me," she said, ushering us back into the room. Once again, we stood in front of the older judge, who reminded me of Zeus on the mountaintop.

"How old did you say you were, Quin?" he asked me.

"Seventy," I responded.

Electricity bolted through my body.

"And you, Misha?" he queried.

"I'm thirty-five."

"This is the deal—I really liked you. We want you to go into another room to dance and be judged again. This time, there will be three judges."

Another audition. Another chance!

"THANK YOU. THANK YOU. THANK YOU!" I remember saying to him.

"Remember this—the camera will be on you from the minute you enter the room. Dance for your life!" he urged us.

The young assistant then walked us out and down another hallway.

"Okay," she said. "Hold on here just a few more minutes."

As we waited with excitement, we watched the other dance contestants leave the building. Their rainbow sequins and glittery costumes reflected rays from the setting sun like mini disco balls as they headed back out into the November air. Then, after some time, the assistant said, "Okay you two, follow me."

The judge's advice stayed in my mind: *"Dance for your life. Act confident as soon as you open the door. Be ready. The cameras are on and focused on you."*

The door opened, and I was determined to show them who Quin was. Confident. Sassy. Fierce. Ready to dance for my life. I had nothing to prove. I only needed to show them who I was.

The three judges in this new room riddled us with questions:

> *How long have you been dancing?*
> *When did you start dancing?*
> *How old are you again?*
> *Tell us about your partnership . . .*

We weren't even sure if we would dance for them because their questions kept coming. I didn't think about it much then, but I now realize they were assessing our chemistry and personalities for the show.

We were funny. We were likeable. We were genuinely ourselves.

After several minutes of talking, the judges finally said, "Show us what you got."

Our music started, and we danced the same routine as we had earlier. Once again, we hit every mark, we soared, and we danced our hearts out.

"Thank you! That was amazing!" the judges said.

ORLANDO AUDITION

Then we followed the assistant into what they called the Story Room. We learned that this was the next step for potential contestants. We were interviewed there for more than an hour by members of the *AGT* writing team. Without any explanation or instruction, with no idea what we were supposed to do or what was going to happen, we told our stories.

We made another trek down a long, winding hallway until we got to a grand ballroom. This space was longer than it was wide—about fifty yards long—with a giant camera on wheels that ran up and down a track. Hundreds of audition contestants were watching us as we entered the room. All eyes were on us. The producer instructed Misha and me to dance with excitement down the length of the room and told us that the camera would follow us, capturing our every move. Almost as soon as she finished explaining, she shouted, "OKAY! GO!"

So we turned on the charm, turned up the energy, and—once again—danced like our lives depended on it. We jumped, leaped, flipped, and frolicked back and forth—smiling and genuinely enjoying every move. The camera tracked us each step of the way. As we ended our routine, the crowd exploded with applause. Months later, we learned that much of that footage ended up on *AGT* commercials promoting Season 13.

Then we were led back into the Story Room, where the *AGT* staff member thanked us for our efforts and told us we'd hear back after the first of the year. We had no idea if we had made it onto the show. We left the building at 9:00 pm, feeling utterly exhausted but thrilled after a full day of dancing for our lives.

We didn't know what to expect. We didn't know what to think.

What I did know is that I felt excited. I knew they liked us. We had done exceptionally well. The attention we got was all extraordinarily positive. Each hallway led us to another doorway, and each door opened for us—giving us a new opportunity to present who we were to people who looked for reasons to eliminate us. We left without elimination, and we were elated.

ORLANDO AUDITION

Three short weeks later, we got a call from an *America's Got Talent* producer, who introduced herself as "our producer" and instructed us to begin "initial preparations" to come to Pasadena, California, for another tryout—this time with the Celebrity Judges.

"I can't promise what the final decision will be," she said. "Just be ready."

And so Misha and I got ready.

CHAPTER 15
CELEBRITY JUDGES

My cellphone rang while Misha and I were training. It was Alexa, the *AGT* producer.

"Hi Alexa," I said, "I'm with Misha. I'll put you on speaker."

"Quin and Misha, I am pleased to tell you that you have been selected to try out for the Celebrity Judges Audition in Pasadena," she said excitedly.

"YES!! That's fantastic news," I screamed. Misha and I high-fived and hugged each other.

She told us that she would be emailing all the specific details to us.

"You must keep everything a secret," she instructed. "You cannot share with anyone that you're talking to me or that we're gathering information from you. Keep everything—every single detail—confidential."

Of course, Misha and I had told our friends and

family, back in November, that we were trying out. A secret like this gets heavy after months of carrying it around. We could not even hint about the results of our Orlando tryouts; we had to repeatedly tell anyone who asked, "We still don't know. We're not sure if we made it through or not."

Meanwhile, our training became very intense, and Rick and I decided that it didn't make sense for me to drive back and forth to Jacksonville each day. So we rented an apartment there. I would drive up on Monday morning and train throughout the week, returning to Orlando on Friday afternoon, giving my body a better chance to recover.

This next round was very different from the first tryout. Everything had to be approved in advance. We could not use the same song, and we had to send a list of song choices, to be approved by the music department. Our dance routine also received feedback, and we needed to make adjustments. For the next two months, we shared rehearsal videos and song choices with our producer, trying to win approval for our song and routine. At the end of every conversation and every email, she would remind us, "Keep everything—every single detail—confidential." We didn't share our happiness with anyone, and I often felt like I was choking on our good news. We were constantly monitored by the AGT producers, whose sole job was to ensure we didn't leak any information about the show.

To get ready for the Celebrity Judges Audition, I

CELEBRITY JUDGES

had to drastically alter the ballroom dress I had worn at the Orlando audition. From the first moment they caught a glimpse of me strutting into the Orange County Convention Center, the producers loved that dress—and it was my favorite dress, too. I had worn it intentionally, because it was a showstopper—hot pink chiffon with flapper-style tassels at the bottom. The skirt catches every move, swirling around my legs and waist with each swing of my hips. The beading on top reflects both light and shadows, beaming magical rays of light as I twist and turn. The dress was a spectacle by itself, and the camera seemed to love it as much as the *AGT* producers did. So it was no surprise that—as a condition of their still-not-finalized decision—the producers required that I wear it for the televised California audition. There was just one problem—the hand-beaded top, dripping with large Swarovski crystal stones, is not meant to be worn for the dangerous lifting moves Misha and I would do in our new routine. The was designed for the Cha-Cha, with a high-choker collar, long sleeves that end with crystal bracelets at the wrist, and a river of crystal stones down my back—not ideal for lifting and twirling moves! In fact, when I wore the dress in Orlando, Misha left the auditions with bloody scratches all over his arms and face. Each time he lifted, twirled, tossed, and caught me, he had suffered what felt, and looked like, a hundred cat scratches on his skin. He had smiled through all of it, but the dress was also heavy and hard for him to lift me in. To really do the moves that Misha and I were planning for Pasadena required a different kind of dress entirely. So I took scissors to the masterpiece myself and—cutting, ripping, and sewing—customized it for a proper AGT audition. I knew that thousands of people in the audience, alongside Simon, Heidi, Mel B, and Howie, would be judging us, and I was determined to impress each one of them. They all mattered!

With my refashioned dress waiting on its padded hanger, we filled our days creating and recreating new choreography, choosing a song the producers would approve, stretching and working out, and tweaking our choreography again. We knew we had to upgrade our routine to include spectacular lifts and spins. So we asked coach Craig Smith to help Misha learn how to lift. During our first session, Craig demonstrated what was possible with spins by lifting my eighty-five-pound body over his head and immediately going into a series of high-speed moves. I had never experienced anything like them before. They were faster than some of the most dangerous rides I had been on at theme parks. My head was still spinning as we left the studio and, pulling out of the parking lot, I asked Misha to pull the car over so I could vomit. For the next few days, my dizziness continued. I went to my family physician to see if there was something wrong, and a neurologist put me through a series of tests, including a brain scan and an MRI. Fortunately, there was no damage, and

CELEBRITY JUDGES

the dizziness went away about a week later. But I knew that the risks would be higher with each practice and performance, as our lifts and spins became increasingly daring.

But we continued to do whatever it took to get to Pasadena in March for televised auditions in front of the celebrity judges. More than seventy-five thousand people tried out for *America's Got Talent*, Season 13, and only the top two hundred acts made it to the celebrity judges' audition. Misha and I were one of those winning acts.

When the day of our journey arrived—March 5, 2018—we left the house at 4:30 am for our five hour, 6:00 am flight. *AGT*, in perpetual control, had made all the travel arrangements for Rick, Misha, and me, and they told Rick, too, to be prepared for on-camera interviews.

The trip to the Orlando International Airport usually takes twenty-five minutes. When we got to the airport parking lot, we boarded a shuttle to transport us to the terminal, and then—quite abruptly—it stopped. With less than two miles between us and our departure gate, the shuttle was stuck. The driver said he had never seen a traffic snarl like it before. As we inched along, centimeter by centimeter, Rick began sweating, and Misha stared with tight lips and wide eyes out the window. I kept my chin up and shoulders back, knowing that we had not come this far for it to be the end of the road. By the time we reached the sidewalk check-in outside the airport, however, it was 5:35 am.

"Sorry, check-in has closed for this flight," the attendant told us.

"No way! We must get on this flight! We're auditioning for *America's Got Talent*," Rick cried out.

"Sorry, you'll have to take another flight," she replied. She had no idea how hard we had worked to get this far and how strict the producers were. Our schedule was packed, with no room for error and almost no time to transition from one activity to the next. Missing our flight would be devastating.

It was way too early in the morning, California-time, to try to reach our *AGT* producer. My head began to spin. Rick looked around anxiously, as if trying to find an answer somewhere. Meanwhile, Misha was talking with great animation to an airline agent. We were scheduled to be picked up at the Los Angeles International Airport at 9:00 am. Our only option was to re-book a flight to L.A. that had a connection and layover in Minnesota, but it wouldn't get us into LAX until 1:00 pm—four hours after our scheduled arrival time.

"Let's do it!" I decided.

We ran down the length of the airport to our new gate and sent our producer a text from the plane before taking off, hoping she would understand. We prayed that we hadn't lost our chance to dance in front of the celebrity judges. We had sacrificed so much to get to this point— literal blood, sweat, and tears. *This cannot be the end of my journey*, I repeated

CELEBRITY JUDGES

over and over to myself during the flight to Minnesota.

When we arrived in Minneapolis, we all checked our phones. The *AGT* producers had called and reassured us, saying, "We will see you when you arrive. Don't worry." With a collective sigh of relief, we took off for L.A.

After arriving at LAX, the *AGT* van picked us up for the ride to Pasadena. At three o'clock in the afternoon, after what felt like a lifetime, we arrived at the Pasadena Civic Auditorium and checked in. Misha and I spent the entire afternoon being interviewed and photographed and learned that we would be the last act performing in the next day's afternoon session.

We had prepared for this performance, nonstop, for three months. Misha and I would dance the Swing to a song, vetted and determined by the producers, called "Something New." Performed by Nicky Yanofsky and written by musicians including Herbie Hancock and Quincy Jones, it was not our first choice. It wasn't even our fifth choice, or our fifteenth. Approved songs had to go through a stringent, critical review by multiple producers before they were green-lighted—and each time they rejected a song, Misha and I had to change our routine, creating new choreography to match another song's beat and story.

Musicality matters to a dancer—it's vital to the success of a performance. Dancers can be technically perfect, but if they don't have musicality—if they can't tell the story with their bodies—then they are ultimately unsuccessful. In the months leading up to our Pasadena auditions, we went through about a dozen rejected songs, which translated into more than a dozen revised choreographed routines and hundreds of practices that ultimately amounted to another rejected dance. Each time we were finally satisfied with our routine, our producer would ask us to alter some move, some small part, and we'd have to make changes and learn a new version. Although we had a skeleton routine down, we had to align the moves and the movement to the story of the song, making continuous changes to match each selected piece.

I knew that my musicality had to evoke awe in the judges. So when "Something New" was finally approved, I listened to the song on repeat for hours and hours every day, for three weeks, so I could embody the lyrics. And Misha worked frantically to create the most important routine of our lives. A genius at choreography, he created an upbeat, lively dance that involved lifts, drops, and footwork that would challenge the most experienced dancer. I had to learn the routine, flawlessly, in about three weeks.

Finally, on Tuesday, March 6, 2018, we checked in with our producer at 9:00 am, although we weren't scheduled to perform until 5:00 pm in the afternoon. We once again spent the entire day being interviewed and photographed, and Rick was interviewed, too. Then, at around 11:00 am, we were ushered onto the

CELEBRITY JUDGES

big stage for our one and only rehearsal. There was no other place for us to practice. Security was zipped up tight—they even followed us into the bathroom. We had no warmup and no music and rehearsed using only muscle memory. Then, as camera angles were checked and re-checked, we watched other acts while we sat in the audience. My eyes flashed to the judges' names suspended in air in big lights, with X's ready to reject any contestant who didn't meet a judge's standards.

By late afternoon, the three of us were ushered outside to have an interview with Tyra Banks as hundreds of spectators began entering the auditorium to take their seats. We then waited in the holding room until the producers sent for us. After what felt like hours more, an *AGT* team member finally led us backstage. No matter what we did, the camera was constantly filming us. The area was dark, cramped, and packed with people. We could hear what was happening on stage, but we couldn't see anything.

Suddenly, Tyra Banks called out:

"Quin and Misha, come!"

And without hesitation with the words of our song ringing in my head, I walked out—as tall as my four-foot-eleven-inch frame could make me—and onto the stage, alongside Misha. Applause from the crowd greeted us, and the four celebrity judges looked at us intently: Simon Cowell, Heidi Klum, Mel B, and Howie Mandel. I took a deep breath, smiled, and looked each judge in the eye.

FEARLESS GIRL

Simon began peppering us with questions about us and our relationship:

"So, who are you?" he asked.

"My name is Misha."

"I'm Quin."

Simon followed up with, "And the name of the group is...."

"Quin and Misha," Misha responded seriously.

The judges, especially Howie, and the audience laughed.

Simon asked, "And are you husband and wife?"

We both said "No" simultaneously.

"What's the relationship?" Simon asked.

I looked at Misha and started to hesitantly answer,

CELEBRITY JUDGES

"It's a……"

At that moment, Mel B looked at Heidi, and the audience responded as though there was something not being stated.

Misha quickly followed up with, "Not in a romantic one."

I said, "Yes."

Simon, thinking he caught me, asked, "You are?"

"No!" I said this time.

The audience laughed and Mel B reinforced to Simon, "No!"

"How old are you?" Simon asked.

"I'm thirty-five," Misha responded.

"I am seventy years old," I announced with pride.

Mel B and Howie screamed out: "No way!"

The crowd howled.

Simon asked unbelievingly, "Are you serious?

I said, "I'll be seventy-one next month."

"You look incredible!" Simon stated.

"Thank you," I replied

"Are you married?" he asked.

"Yes," I responded and pointed to Rick standing backstage, "He's back there. I danced with him for three years, and I said to myself that I think I'm going to look for a younger guy to dance with."

The judges and the audience roared with laughter.

"And he's happy about this?" Simon asked.

"He told Tyra today that he was making an adjustment," I replied.

More laughter.

Simon then asked to see Rick and greeted him when he walked out at the back of the stage. "Nice to meet you, sir."

Soon, he signaled us to begin, saying, "I'm excited. Good luck."

Misha and I took our positions, and the first beats of "Something New" boomed through the auditorium. All I cared about was giving the audience a good show—we didn't want to let anyone down. Our goal was to turn up the volume physically to match the energy we felt inside. We wanted our moves to be organic but to also look larger than life. I wanted to make every eye in the audience watch me!

We went in thinking, *This is our one time. We have nothing to lose.* No nerves at all. Just pure excitement. In what felt like a flash, our one-minute-and-forty-five-second Swing performance dramatically ended with Misha spinning me over his head and into a death drop. Spontaneously, I blew a big kiss to the judges as I hung sideways, Misha still holding tightly to my left wrist. The auditorium erupted in a standing ovation, including all of the four judges. Misha and I hugged each other tightly, knowing we had crushed our performance.

"Thank you, guys," Simon exclaimed. "A standing ovation! What do you think?"

It was time for the judges to give us their feedback and vote to decide if we would make it through to the next round.

I was overjoyed.

CELEBRITY JUDGES

"I mean, your kicks! And you're so toned! It is nuts! You don't have an expiration date, and you just showed that. And I love what you just did," Heidi exclaimed earnestly.

"I loved it!" Mel B said and then asked us, "Moving forward, if you were to go to the next round, do you do different styles of dance?"

Misha and I excitedly responded together, "Yes, all different styles of dance – waltz, tango, …"

And Howie Mandel jokingly interrupted, "I love it that the thirty-five-year-old is out of breath."

"How long have you been doing this?" Howie asked.

"I started out when I was sixty. Our son's friend was getting married, and I don't know how to move…"

He interrupted "… Oh yes you do! And as a married guy, if my wife moved like you, I'd need an adjustment too."

The audience broke out in laughter again.

"You know what's so great about you two," Simon continued, "is you're interesting. And I think you are inspirational, which is important. I think it was a great audition!"

My breath caught in my chest with excitement. The feedback and the laughter felt so good!

"Okay, I think it's time to vote!" Simon directed, "Howie?"

"YES!" Howie exclaimed.

"YESSSSSSSS!!!" Mel B proclaimed.

Oh my gosh, I could not believe this was happening!

"Yes!" Heidi smiled and gave us the thumbs-up sign.

"Okay, Quin and Misha, you got four yeses. Congratulations!! You are going on to the next round," Simon said with a smile.

We hugged again, and as I kissed Misha and we

CELEBRITY JUDGES

walked off the stage, hand in hand, we overheard Howie say to the other judges, "That's amazing, just freakish. I can't touch my toes." Rick was waiting backstage for us with Tyra Banks and we all hugged. We savored this incredible moment.

When you watch the video of our audition, you'll see us leaving the stage with Fun's song "We Are Young" playing in the background. The post-production crew must have felt our energy—the energy of the entire room—after our performance. I relished every second of it with the same thrill I had experienced listening to voices over father's plastic radio as a girl, leaving my village on foot to seek new opportunities and flying across oceans to America to marry Rick. Every event in my extraordinary life had led me to this moment. My dreams, once cocooned in empty darkness, had been realized onstage, in front of thousands of people, four celebrity judges, and cameras capturing our every move—and they would soon be televised to millions of viewers at home.

Afterwards, when the three of us left the auditorium to get something to eat, we were recognized by many people, on the streets and in the restaurant, who had seen the performance.

"You two are amazing," one person said. "Good luck in the next round!" another chimed in. That night, I burned brighter than the sun. I was forever young!

The last person we had spoken to before we left the theater was the attorney for *AGT*. He said, "In order to move forward, you're going to have to sign this contract." It spelled out quite clearly the rules and policies that Misha and I had to follow. We were legally bound to keep everything confidential and allow *AGT* to control everything leading up to the live shows—from our music to our costumes, the dance routines, interviews on TV and magazines, and even what we posted on social media. Misha and I were no longer considered "independent" performers; we were members of the *AGT* cast. The entire process now changed dramatically. We had to send in more than fifteen songs for consideration, and we finally had to take their suggestion for a fast, feisty, upbeat song called "Sax," by Fleur East, that was completely unknown to us. But with Misha's choreographic mastery, we were able to adapt moves that felt organic and authentic to the music chosen by the *AGT* producers.

They also needed to approve the choreography, and we had to submit videos for approval. They might say, "We like the routine, but it needs more lifts and spins," or "it needs more dancing." We spent hours and hours learning new moves, only to hear that more changes had to be made. Misha altered our routine time after time. When we finally got approval for the song and our routine, we only had three weeks to perfect it, even though we would normally spend half a year doing that.

Dancers rely on feeling and muscle memory to achieve control, and we had to make our dance look

CELEBRITY JUDGES

effortless. The Judge's Cut round would be the most important routine we would ever dance – a seemingly once-in-a-lifetime opportunity. The challenge seemed overwhelming, but we chose to adapt and find a way to make it happen.

Our response was always, "We'll do it!"

CHAPTER 16
THE GOLDEN BUZZER

To this day, I can still hear Howie Mandel's voice in my head, as he introduced Misha and me for the Judges' Cut round. One month after our Pasadena audition, when we were standing on the Universal Studios stage, in front of hundreds of people and with TV cameras rolling from every angle, he declared, "Only seven acts are going through tonight . . . We wish you the best of luck." And then, "Take the stage . . . it's yours."

And for about two minutes, the stage was ours. We wanted a jaw-dropping ballroom routine, so we included spins, lifts, and dazzling drops that we had never done before, hoping we could move the judges and the audience off their seats and onto their feet.

But the reality is, we almost didn't make it—not to the Judge's Cut round, not to Los Angeles, and not to the end of our routine. The unthinkable happened.

FEARLESS GIRL

I had just received a new dance costume from my dress designers, four days before the performance. Although *America's Got Talent* has its own wardrobe team that makes costumes for everyone, they advised me to bring my own costume in case I didn't like what they provided or it didn't fit well. That was fine with me, because I loved my ballroom gown designers—two gifted women who had also created costumes for *Dancing with the Stars*. We wanted my costume to be dazzling, and they created a matching costume for Misha.

The day before we were scheduled to fly out to LA, we thought we should go through a dress rehearsal to make sure we were comfortable in our new costumes. We went through the routine once slowly, with exaggerated movements in slow motion. And then we decided to rehearse again at full speed.

That's when it happened. One wrong step, in exactly the wrong spot.

Misha's foot came stomping down on mine, like he was crushing out a cigarette against concrete. Searing pain knocked the wind out of me, and I watched in horror as something red flew across the floor.

It was my crimson-painted middle toenail.

No, no, no!

Like a scene from a scary movie, blood from my toe spurted everywhere. I couldn't get it to stop. I was wearing fishnet stockings and high heels with open toes, and the blood seeped through relentlessly. Tears

THE GOLDEN BUZZER

stung my throat and eyes as I realized that this injury would likely end our *AGT* dreams. After all our training, the traveling, the new apartment, and the excitement—the life-changing excitement—how could our dream end like this?

We headed straight to the closest Urgent Care. They rushed me in to see the doctor, but he told me, "This is too severe for me to do anything here. You

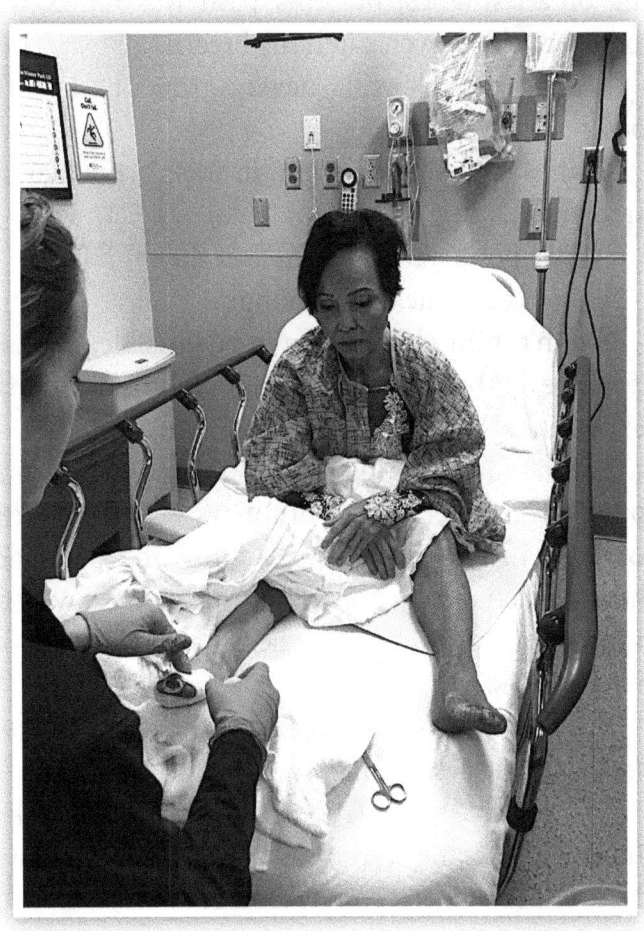

need to go to the hospital." So we piled back into the car and sped to the hospital emergency room, where we stayed for the next four hours. The attending physician injected a numbing agent straight into my toe, then cleaned and taped it up tightly while I choked back screams. The injection hadn't fully numbed me, and pain jolted every nerve in my body. I'd been through so much in my life without medicine or anesthetics, but this pain was among the worst. I couldn't even catch my breath.

"Your toenail will never grow back," the doctor said.

That was bad news, but it wasn't the news I cared about.

"Will I be able to dance in four days?" I asked.

He looked at me disbelievingly.

"I don't think that's going to be possible," he said. "It may even be difficult for you to walk during the next week."

I didn't say anything else. The nurse pumped me up with painkillers and sent me off with a prescription and instructions for changing the bandages. Then they left us to gather up our things and wait for the orderly to arrive with a wheelchair to take me out to the car.

How quickly life can change, I thought. *Treasure what you have when you have it.*

On the drive home, I was in shock. I didn't look at Misha or Rick and didn't say a word. I just knew it was over because the pain was so bad.

THE GOLDEN BUZZER

Once we got home, nobody spoke. We were all stunned. I got into bed for a few hours, but the painkillers had worn off, and I couldn't get any sleep. In the morning, when I tried to get out of bed, I couldn't even stand up, so I crawled out of the bedroom to the living room. Rick and Misha were there, watching me in stunned silence.

"We'll have to call the producer and tell her you can't come," Rick finally concluded, sadly.

"But there's no point in calling her now," Misha remarked, "because she's probably still asleep in California."

Everyone sat silently for another ten minutes.

Suddenly I said, "Let's go!"

"Honey, you can't perform in this condition!" Rick said.

"Will you please carry me into the car? We're already packed," I said.

Rick and Misha looked at each other in disbelief. Then Rick said to him, "When she makes up her mind, I follow."

"It might be best if we go there and talk to the producers in person," Misha agreed.

But in my heart, I couldn't imagine giving up. It was as if I was saying to God, *You brought me this far. This can't be the end.*

When we reached the airport, Rick arranged for a porter with a wheelchair to transport me to the gate. Misha and I would fly out together now, and Rick would be joining us the next day.

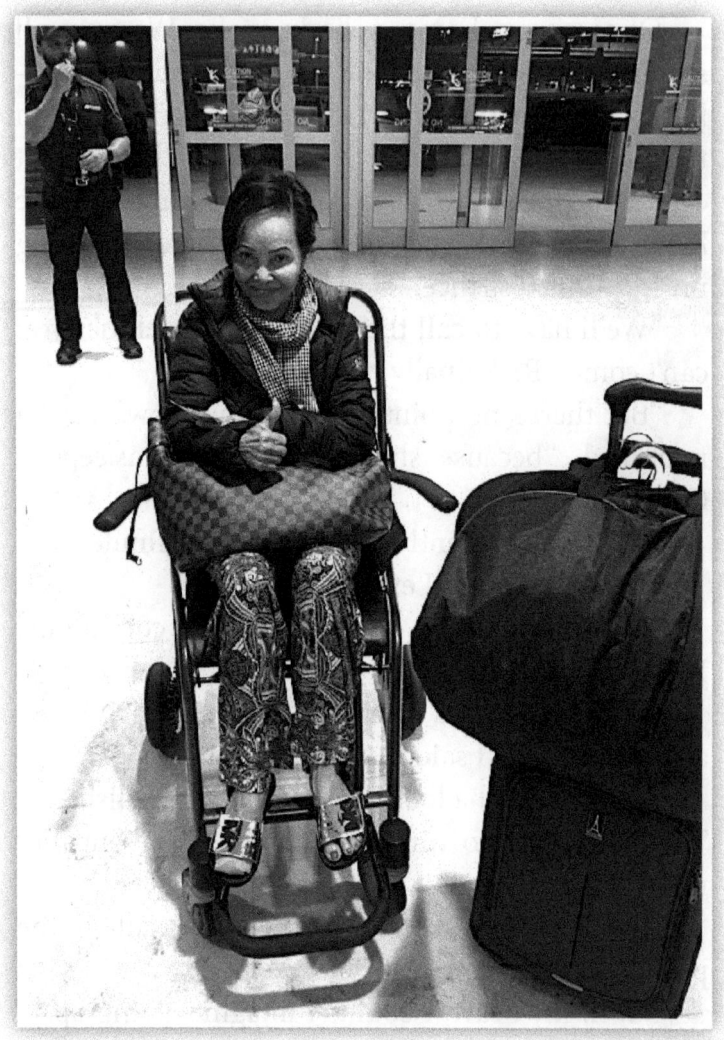

During the five-hour flight, I tried to keep my foot elevated, but by the time we arrived in Los Angeles, all I wanted to do was crawl into a bed and stay there until it was healed. That was hardly possible. *AGT* had sent a van to pick us up and take us to the

THE GOLDEN BUZZER

hotel to check in. After dropping us off, it would return in two hours to take us to Universal Studios.

I called our coach, Michael Chapman. Misha and I had gone to him for coaching after the Orlando audition, and he choreographed our dance for the Judge's Cut round. In addition to being a talented and creative choreographer, Michael is a very compassionate and wise soul. I explained what had happened and asked him what I should do.

"Quin, don't tell them yet how bad it is," he said in a caring, concerned voice. "It's very possible that you'll feel a little bit better tomorrow and each day after."

I also texted one of my friends, Denise Namen, whose husband was a foot doctor. I told her what was going on, and she asked me to send a photo of my foot so she could show it to her husband. I removed my bandage, snapped the picture, and texted it. It had been almost twenty-four hours since my injury, and blood was still flowing. Instructions came back in five minutes— "Soak your foot in a bath with Epsom salt and vinegar. This will help stop the bleeding."

By this time, the van had returned and taken us to the studio, where our producer, Alexa, met us.

"Hey! How are you guys?"

"Well, we've had a little accident…" Misha explained. "Quin's toe is injured."

"How bad is it?"

"Not too bad," I lied. "I think if you could just give us an extra day before we have to dance, it will be okay."

"Okay, no dancing for you today or tomorrow," she said and sent us back to the hotel to rest. "Tomorrow, we'll pick you up and just do some interviews and filming."

I was relieved. I had been afraid to tell her how bad it was, worried that she would think it too risky and replace us with another act. But if I still couldn't dance in two days, I would have to ask her if we had any options. All four judges had given us a standing ovation when we performed at the first taped show in Pasadena—and that, I felt, had to count for something. Maybe they could have us come back the following week.

When we got back to the hotel room, I soaked my foot and then kept it elevated. But the bleeding still hadn't fully stopped the next day when the *AGT* crew picked us up and drove us to a distant location.

"We're going to do some scenery shots here of you dancing," a crew member explained.

Dancing? But I'm not supposed to dance today, I thought.

The producer wasn't there—it was just us and the camera crew, and I didn't know what to do other than go along with what they asked for. We had to cut my old open-toe dance shoe to enable me to slide my foot in with the bandage around it. I wound up on my feet almost the entire day, and it was unbearable. But I still wasn't ready to give up. Misha thought I was crazy, but he went along with me. Mind over matter.

THE GOLDEN BUZZER

I was still breathing and was not going to give up.

By the third day, the bleeding had stopped, unless I put pressure directly on my foot. We practiced our routine on stage so that the crew could set the lighting and camera angles. It was terrible to dance on my foot, but there was no time to modify our routine at all to compensate for my injury. All the acts that day were amazing. It would be difficult to compete against them under normal circumstances, since many of them already had large social media followings and lots of experience on camera. We were the underdogs, but I stayed focused, knowing that Misha and I had worked as hard as anyone on that show to be there.

I kept telling myself, *Mind over matter. You can do it.* We walked to the holding room to join the other contestants before performing. In the contestant meeting, one of the *AGT* executives told us, "If you make it through this round, your life will be changed forever!" There were more cameras in that room than you could imagine. Nearly every moment of our time on *AGT* was filmed or photographed. We had microphones on all throughout our practice days because producers were always looking for new angles, new stories, and banter between the acts. We became so familiar with the interview and film team that they began endearingly calling me "Quinspire," because they said they felt inspired each time we met.

During the Judge's Cut performances, producers moved the other contestants around backstage and encouraged us to talk to each other so they could film

FEARLESS GIRL

our reactions to the auditions. That was hard sometimes because many artists turn inward when they're nervous. All the contestants who hadn't performed yet, even seasoned performers, were trying to focus and tamp down their stage fright. We were chatty at mealtimes, but rehearsals and performances were naturally quieter times. I was in so much pain, I didn't even think about getting nervous. I did my best to stay positive and engage with my fellow contestants. I knew it was important to be brave, even when I wasn't in the spotlight.

"Quin and Misha! You're up next—let's go!" a producer said suddenly. After the paradox of what felt like forever and the blink of an eye, it was our big moment—our time to walk out on stage in front of the live audience and the five celebrity judges.

At the start of each performance, *AGT* showed a highly edited version of interview clips, telling whatever piece of our story they wanted to tell that week. For this performance, our video montage showed the story of how I'd met Rick forty-six years earlier and had come to live in America. I heard myself exclaiming, "I'm so grateful every day to live in this country. I still appreciate it every day." The producers had edited the video so that it showed the story of my upbringing in Thailand and how Rick and I met, then jumped to how I learned ballroom dancing and how much it meant to me. The video continued with me emphasizing, "Misha and I have been dancing together for the past five years. We have been working

THE GOLDEN BUZZER

so hard to go to the Live Show because I want to show the world that 'Hey, listen, just because you're sixty or seventy, don't sit there.'" It concluded with me saying, "If we won *America's Got Talent,* it would mean the world to me."

As the video concluded, I heard, "Okay, you're on!"

With my wrapped toe and cut-up shoe, I got out on that stage with Misha and thought, *This is it. I'm going to give it every ounce of strength I have. If I pass out or even die on that stage, at least I'll die famous.*

It was certainly the place to do it! We were seconds away from performing on one of the most-watched televised programs in the entire world, and it was surreal. For a moment, the memory of crouching over a transistor radio in a hut with my family flashed before my eyes.

We had impressed the four regular judges before,

and now the panel included guest judge and country star Martina McBride.

Howie said, "Quin and Misha, welcome back. For those that don't know, your age is......"

"I'm seventy-one!" I said proudly.

The judges looked at each other nodding their heads.

"Only seven acts are going through. Is there a lot of pressure back there?" Howie asked.

"Yes!" I said.

"Are you excited?" he followed up.

"Yes, we are so excited," I emphasized.

Continuing, Howie said, "You found a young partner. You're a married woman. This is not your husband."

'No," Misha responded.

"But you're still happily married, right?" Howie queried.

"Oh, yes!" I said in all seriousness. "And he supports us 150 percent."

With that, the introductory video was played.

As it ended, Howie said, "We wish you the best of luck..." and then, "Take the stage... it's yours."

As our music started, I focused on smiling and hitting my choreography with precision. The adrenaline kicked in and, even though I still felt searing pain, I refused to allow it to take center stage. Instantly, the pain faded; the rush of performing took over and served as a powerful painkiller! Soon I was upside down, spinning around in the air and on the

THE GOLDEN BUZZER

floor, doing a split, feeling the flashing spotlights, and vibrating music all around us, hearing the audience cheer, and feeling the rush of the audience's support, knowing that I was defying stereotypes with every audacious move.

I had a moment of clarity while spinning above Misha's head—*I can't believe we are doing this!* Ours was no ordinary ballroom dance routine, of course—the producers wanted something much flashier and more dangerous than that. I was pushing way past my comfort zone and doing more on stage in my seventies than most people do in their entire adult lives. The performance went by in a flash, into the last movement of our routine, where Misha swung me around six times and shot me forward on the floor, toward the judges and into our final pose. The music stopped. The audience erupted. Misha helped me to my feet so we could compose ourselves and hear the judge's reactions.

"You have definitely inspired me. I think you're an absolutely incredible woman. I love what you do. I love watching you guys. I'm very impressed," said Heidi Klum.

I felt relief flood my body—a great start!

"The best part about you guys is your personality. Every time you come on, you light up the stage. This was great. This is what we're looking for," Simon exulted.

Then came Martina's turn, and she was staring into my eyes. For a moment, I worried that she was looking at my feet—I thought maybe my toe had bled through the bandage again, or perhaps the tape had unraveled. I was trying not to show that I was rattled and didn't want to look down to check, but I didn't know how to read Martina's face.

Howie had buzzed a dance act earlier in the show, and it made all the contestants edgy. Once we made it past the auditions and the first judges' round, we figured that everyone was talented enough to stay in the competition without being buzzed, but tonight it had happened when Howie felt disappointment. And

THE GOLDEN BUZZER

that's what I thought had happened—maybe my injury had harmed the performance, in her view, more than I realized.

"Wow, you know you say you want to inspire people of a certain age. But you inspired everybody of all ages. A truly remarkable performance," she said.

Looking at the other judges, Martina followed with, "I don't know. It just really moved me! I think it's incredible. So...."

She leaned in, and though my eyes blurred, I could see that she was reaching.

And then...

A shower of confetti rained down on us in golden light, and I realized what had just happened: MARTINA PRESSED HER GOLDEN BUZZER FOR US!!

My heart raced and my legs buckled. I dropped to my knees on the stage and wept with joy. Everything was a blur; it was happening so quickly, and yet I knew this was a moment I would replay in my mind for the rest of my life.

In that moment, I had more than I had ever dreamed about in life. My husband, who had loved and supported me for forty-six years, was celebrating in the audience. My best dance partner was next to me. And we had just been recognized on national television as the act Martina McBride thought was the best of the night. I was so overwhelmed with complete and total gratitude; I instinctively gave the world my Thai *wai*.

FEARLESS GIRL

Memories, like the bits of gold that rained down all around me, raced through my mind — my parents, who struggled to keep their family alive through starvation and poverty; my siblings, some of whom had not survived; my extended family in Thailand, who would soon watch me as I represented our motherland; my friends in Florida, some of whom had supported me from my first years in America; and my son and grandchildren, who represented the future for us all. I saw the face of my dance coach, beaming with pride, and the fans who had sent me such beautiful notes of support. I saw a flash of Rick as a young soldier, begging me to come with him to a new country and be his wife, and all the seniors who would watch this moment and realize that it wasn't too late for them to push past their boundaries and do something crazy, too. But mostly, I thought about eight-year-old Kim and how far she had come to become this woman, in a black-and-white sequined costume, who was now named Quin—how it was a miracle that she had even survived to be in this moment, bathed in golden light.

I gathered up some of the gold pieces from the stage; it felt like a message straight from heaven, encouraging me to keep going. I wanted to touch it, to hold it forever. *Thank you, God!*

As I stood, stunned, shimmering under the stage lights, I knew that no one could see the scars I bore, both literal and figurative. The marks from a childhood filled with danger, infection, and starvation.

THE GOLDEN BUZZER

The emotional turmoil of leaving my home and family in search of a better life in a new country whose language I'd barely begun to learn. My deep loneliness and longing for my family. The crushing end of my life on the courts. The search for spiritual wholeness and a sense of purpose in serving others. In that moment, so much that had been hurting inside of me mended. I realized that the third act of my life might be the best one yet. I didn't want to leave that stage.

Everyone in the theater, including the judges, was on their feet, applauding and cheering us. Martina McBride came onstage to embrace us. Tyra Banks shouted as she hugged us, "Quin and Misha are going straight to the Live Show!"

Rick was waiting backstage for us, and Misha and I ran into his arms as we all cried. "This is unbelievable," he said.

When the show aired on TV on July 31, 2018, it showed the judges backstage afterwards, chatting about our performance.

"You have a very inspiring Golden Buzzer," Howie commented to Martina.

"Yes, there's so many people that kind of give up at a certain point in their life. I really think Quin's message is something so many people can benefit from hearing," Martina said.

The next morning, my social media accounts exploded with energy. Facebook instantly filled up, and I received texts and emails by the minute. One of my nieces from Bangkok phoned me, saying, with astonishment, "Auntie, your picture and the Golden Buzzer are on every TV station and newspaper in Thailand!" A photo of me giving the *wai* was circulated worldwide immediately after the show aired. With the global exposure and, especially, the excited interest in Thailand, I was interviewed by many media outlets, including the BBC in Thailand, *Good Housekeeping*, AARP, the *Daily Mail*, and numerous others. All the TV stations in Thailand requested interviews.

When you spend your childhood urgently trying to survive the circumstances in which you live, you almost instinctively embark on a lifelong quest for control and choice. As a little girl, I had one piece of clothing and often went days without eating. We had no electricity or running water. I had four years of education before working, sunrise to sunset, on my family's land. Choice wasn't a concept I had until I decided to leave my village behind and make a better life for myself. And I didn't know what choice was until after I came to America to marry Rick.

At age sixty, I chose to dance. I love dancing. It allows me to express my feelings without speaking. I have often said, "I dance to live; I don't live to dance." I choose my diet, my habits, and all the things that matter to me as an elite athlete. Both Heidi Klum and Martina McBride praised me for inspiring people of all ages to take risks, to be bold, and to choose joy.

THE GOLDEN BUZZER

Think about it this way—many kids in America today get to choose what they eat for dinner, what they wear to school, who they sit with at lunch, what kind of phone to have. Many kids can decide what high school classes to take, what sports to play, and where to apply to go to college. Some of the more fortunate ones can choose which country they will travel to for spring break, what new car to buy, or even what kind of designer dog to purchase.

I didn't have any of those choices. But as the golden confetti rained down around Misha and me, I felt privileged beyond measure.

I was seen. I was somebody. I mattered. I felt like I had reached heaven itself. It was the celebration of everything I had overcome and every bit of work it had taken to get to that point. The Golden Buzzer moment was a culmination of years of choices that I made—thousands and thousands of decisions that included sacrifice and physical injury; great risks and life-altering acts of defiance; relentless practice; and unyielding perseverance.

My purpose had grown wings.

I was ready to fly.

CHAPTER 17

ADAPT

The Golden Buzzer performance was recorded on April 17, 2018, three months before it would be aired in July. During that time, we were sworn to secrecy and could not tell anyone about our experience. This was extremely difficult since we were so proud that we would be going to the Quarterfinals and the Live Show.

We had four months to get ready for our Live Show performance on August 22. Although this was more time than we had had to prepare for earlier rounds, the Live Show was a major production, and the level of preparation was multiplied many times.

The first item on the *AGT* preparation list was the "home visit." The producers would be sending a film crew to Orlando to film us on June 24. *AGT* planned every detail, from site locations to wardrobes and people to be interviewed. The producers asked Misha and me to send photos of our homes, cars, and sets of casual clothes. They would not decide until later if we would be filming in both Orlando and Jacksonville or only in Orlando. Because we were now part of the *AGT* cast, we fully accepted that we needed to adapt to any request or instruction.

Ultimately, the producers chose Orlando as the only location. Filming would take place at four sites there—a university fitness center, college tennis courts, the dance studio, and my home. They insisted on interviewing my three grandchildren—the eldest, who lives in Orlando, and my twin grandchildren in Chicago, who would have to be flown in.

It was a full day of filming, beginning at 7:30 am at the University of Central Florida fitness center. *AGT* rented the whole facility, so we were the only ones there. For the next three hours, I was filmed stretching, lifting weights, working on various machines, and running track. Next, we traveled across town to the Rollins College tennis courts, where I was filmed playing tennis for the next two hours. The film crew and director had me hit serves, backhands, and forehands and play points in the ninety-five-degree Florida sun.

After a short lunch break, we traveled to the Crystal Ballroom dance studio, where Misha and I were filmed dancing for the next few hours. By late afternoon, we were ready for the last segment at my home. My three grandchildren were interviewed for another hour, and we finally said goodbye to the *AGT* crew at 7:00 pm. I was completely worn out, but I couldn't wait to see what they would do with the

ADAPT

many hours of film they had captured. The edited version would be used for the Live Show, and I was so excited about the possibility of my grandchildren appearing on national television.

It was nearly the end of June, and time was passing quickly. Our coach, Michael Chapman, had met with us to talk about dance routines, song selections, and the stage setting. *AGT* would be creating a massive set specifically for our routine. Misha is a talented artist and sketched out a concept. We sent it, along with ten song suggestions, to the producer, hoping that would speed the decision so we could start serious preparations. Soon after the home visit, *AGT* sent us a mock-up of what the stage set would look like. It had a beach look to it with palm trees, a tiki bar, a tanning booth, and vibrant lighting. We then had a conference call with the creative team's executive producer. Prior to the call, we were sent After sharing our ideas, we agreed to start working on a swing routine and would send more song possibilities for review.

For the next several weeks, we sent videos of our practice sessions to the producer for feedback. Then, in mid-July, less than a month before we would travel to Hollywood, we received the final confirmation of the song choice. It was "Maniac" from the movie *Flashdance*. Although this song had not been our choice, we instantly shifted our mindset to adapt and find a way to work with it. If this was what *AGT* wants, we would give it to them. We could now focus on creating a routine that would be exciting and memorable.

For the Live Show, the *AGT* producers wanted us to raise our danger level to the maximum degree. So we inserted a new lift in what *AGT* judge Heidi Klum called the "death drop." In this lift, when I was completely upside down over Misha's head, he would suddenly drop me, stopping me from falling just inches before my head smashed into the floor. It is a very scary move to watch—and perform. In fact, during a practice session for this lift, our timing was off, and my head banged hard onto the floor. I felt numb and nearly passed out. Misha and I were both frantic, thinking I might have a concussion. I immediately rushed to the doctor's office, and he sent me for an MRI and a CAT scan. With God's Grace, thankfully, the results came back with no damage,

ADAPT

but our confidence was completely jarred. The next day, we flew to New Orleans to perform a show at the Millennium Dance competition. Although we had decided to take the death drop out of the routine, when the music began and our adrenaline peaked, we charged into the performance and the move without a hitch.

On August 13, we arrived in Hollywood to begin preparing for the Live show. The next ten days consisted of rehearsals, wardrobe fittings, social media interviews, choreography consults, reality shoots, and more rehearsals. Each day was a whirlwind of activities beginning at 8:00 am. We were blessed that Michael, our coach, was there with us. It gave us so much confidence and comfort. He quickly established relationships with the executive producer and the choreographers. This proved extremely valuable, since *AGT* made so many changes to our performance, right up to the day before the Live Show. Had Michael not been there with us, it would have been overwhelming.

This time, the *AGT* creative team took care of our wardrobe. They fitted me with a glittery silver, high-necked leotard that looked more like a Jane Fonda-type bathing suit than a ballroom dance costume. The producers dressed Misha in a strange looking T-shirt with white pants. This was definitely not our preferred look. Ballroom dancers everywhere know that costume is just as important as music choice. But Misha and I had become accustomed to

FEARLESS GIRL

ADAPT

adapting. This was *AGT*'s show. They paid for everything from the moment we started, and we were part of the cast.

A few days before the Live Show, there was a major media blitz, and Misha and I were interviewed on the popular TV entertainment news show *Access Hollywood*. Winning the Golden Buzzer had brought us a lot of attention, and before our interview, we waited in a dressing room with a star on the door. It felt surreal.

With the outpouring of attention in Thailand, we were also invited to the Royal Thai Consulate in Los Angeles. We accepted and arranged to visit one day between rehearsals. Consul General Mr. Tanee Sangrat and Lieutenant Consul Gunpirom Vichathorn sent a limo to pick us up and very graciously complimented me on my accomplishments.

FEARLESS GIRL

Consul General Tanee expressed how proud he was of what I was doing and the exposure it was bringing to our homeland. He told us about the Thailand Foundation in Bangkok, which serves to increase knowledge and understanding about Thailand, its people, and its culture. Recently, the consul general told me, he had received a message from the chairman of the foundation asking for examples of Thais who were living in America and doing extraordinary things— "like participating on *America's Got Talent.*" A month later, he added, he learned about me. "This was more than a coincidence," he declared— "You showed up right before my very eyes." While we are at the consulate, he quickly organized his team to video a message of him encouraging all Thai citizens who lived in the United States to vote for us. He introduced me, Misha, and Rick in the video, and I made a few comments expressing my gratitude to all the Thai people who had reached out to me. The consul general circulated the video to all the Thai consulates in America and the Bangkok headquarters of the Thailand Foundation. Afterwards, he presented us with special gifts and took us to Thai Town for lunch. Before we returned to the *AGT* set, I invited Consul General Tanee and his wife to the Live Show, and while riding back to the hotel that day, I thought to myself, *Who would ever believe that the little girl from the rice farm would one day would be invited to meet with a top Thai official in America?*

On August 20, we had our dress rehearsal in the

ADAPT

spectacular Dolby Theater, home of the Academy Awards. The stage is massive, and when we saw our set, we were awestruck by how dynamic it was—like a futuristic movie set. Misha and I took our positions and went through the performance, not missing a beat or step. The crew applauded as confetti rained down on us after I pulled a chain at the end of our dance—a nod to the moment in *Flashdance* when the star dancer pulls a chain and water soaks her.

We were ready!

CHAPTER 18
THE LIVE SHOW

We received VIP tickets for our special guests, and Lukasz, my first coach, flew in from Orlando with his daughter, Lea, to bring us support. It touched my heart deeply that he traveled all the way to watch us perform. He told me that he would never miss the chance to see his student dance on Hollywood's biggest stage. Mr. Tony Tang, who owns the prestigious Ohio Star Ball competition, came to root us on, along with Michael and one of his best friends, Mary Murphy. Mary is one of the stars of the popular TV show, *So You Think You Can Dance*, and through ballroom dance competitions over the years, she and I, too, became friends. When Mary came to wish us well backstage, the other contestants instantly recognized her and rushed to take selfies with her.

As the show began, we were ushered into the holding room with the other contestants, and we all cheered loudly for each other as we watched the performances on a large wall monitor.

FEARLESS GIRL

"Two minutes, Quin and Misha! You're up next. Follow me, please!" the *AGT* production assistant suddenly said, leading us backstage. I took my spot on the million-dollar set, while Misha went in the opposite direction to take his position. The stage lights were off, and as I looked out into the massive, five-tiered theater, the spotlights were shining brightly on the four famous, familiar judges. I could make out only the first row of the audience because of the blazing floodlights. The screams and applause from the audience began to build like a wave as Master of Ceremonies Tyra Banks introduced us.

Every ounce of my body was tingling with excitement. In a few seconds, the first notes of "Maniac" would play, and I would be performing on Hollywood's biggest stage at the world-famous Dolby Theater, with a standing-room-only audience and 17 million TV viewers. I closed my eyes and prayed, but

THE LIVE SHOW

I felt strangely calm. This was the chance of a lifetime, and we were about to show the world what we could do. I was performing on America's #1 watched variety show, *America's Got Talent*, at age seventy-one.

A video began playing that introduced us to the world, although I was not able to see or hear it. Then, with the first beat of the song, Misha charged out of the tanning both, came over, and picked me up, and we plunged into our routine. With our crazy moves and high throws, I looked like a maniacal, futuristic whirlwind. A minute and fifty-two seconds later, with the pull of the chain and white confetti showering us, Misha and I held our final pose, as the audience roared and everyone, including three judges—Simon, Heidi, and Mel B, rose to their feet, applauding and cheering wildly. Then Tyra Banks called us to center stage for the judges' comments.

Heidi began: "I think you are incredible. You're an inspiration. You really, really are. You're twirling on his head, there was a death drop in there. You don't stop and you didn't miss a beat. I thought it was fantastic. You show us that age is just a number."

Simon: "Tonight is one of those nights where we're seeing people and things doing things that they shouldn't do. And that was an example because you are really, really fun. We must take your age into account. You inspire people and I hope you go through to the next round."

Howie: "That's the thing. It's amazing what you're doing for your age. But that's qualifying it. Aside from your age, I don't know if it's worthy enough for moving on."

Heidi and Mel B cut in: "Boo, Howie!" There were boos from the audience, too.

Mel B continued: "You know that movie *Weird Science*? It's like somebody created you. You're not human. You're not normal. What you do is incredible, regardless of your age or not. You kill it on the dance floor, whether you're twenty-two or seventy. Well, done!"

And the voting began.

After the show, we went directly to the red-carpet media event, where dozens of entertainment and celebrity reporters lined up to interview us for the next two hours. It was such an honor to listen to the many compliments Misha and I received on our performance. As we walked down the long,

THE LIVE SHOW

red-carpeted hallway, I felt a glimpse of what it must be like to be at the Academy Awards.

Afterwards, we joined all our guests for an amazing celebration dinner at an upscale Italian restaurant next to the Dolby Theater. I am so grateful to everyone who came to cheer for us in person. It was an overwhelming evening, and my head was spinning from all the excitement.

The Results Show was the following evening, when we would find out if we would go on to the semi-finals. The acts were grouped in threes, and our group included Yumbo Dump, a comedy duo from Japan, and the singer/guitarist Noah Guthrie—known for his pivotal role as Roderick Meeks in the final season of *Glee*. Since the voting was done only by the American public, social media exposure was essential. Most of the acts were professional entertainers and had millions of followers already. Misha and I were a pure amateur team, and our social media campaign had launched only a few months earlier. Because people outside of the U.S. were not permitted to vote, the millions of people in Thailand who wanted to vote for us were unable to do so. We did not advance to the semi-finals—but Misha and I felt like we had won.

I am so thankful to Misha for all that he did for me and his positive attitude on each step of our journey. Michael's incredible coaching and wisdom was also invaluable to us, as he guided us through the rapid changes and intense activity leading up to our final performance. Above all, I am grateful to everyone involved on the *America's Got Talent* team. From the producers to the judges, the writing team, the interviewers, the photographers, the film crew, and the hundreds of stagehands, I will always remember their gracious hospitality and kindness. It has especially been a privilege for me to meet the other contestants and bond together as a family as we faced the many challenges together on TV's #1 variety show.

AGT was an amazing once-in-a-lifetime experience, and I will treasure it forever.

PART 3
POWER

"My power comes from the spirit inside me!"

~ Quin

CHAPTER 19

FOREVER YOUNG

Going all the way to the Live Show on *AGT* was beyond my wildest imagination. I began getting fan mail every day on social media, with heartfelt messages from all over the world, expressing what an inspiration I was to those who saw me perform. I realized that I had found my purpose. Just by being me, I was able to show people that they can do whatever it takes to live a life fulfilled.

What's next? That was the question that was at the top of my mind. It's hard to know where to land after a mountain-top experience like *America's Got Talent*. Each step of our journey with the show was truly extraordinary. Misha and I weren't quite sure how to come back down from the heights we had experienced. We were pioneers in a sense—the first Pro-Am ballroom dance team ever to make it to America's most popular variety show, then advance all the way to the Live Show, winning the Golden Buzzer while competing against professional entertainers from around the world.

One day, I received an offer from a healthcare company to travel to Salt Lake City to help open a new facility for seniors. Its executives had watched me on *AGT* and realized I could perfectly symbolize what's possible for others. They invited me to be a company spokesperson for a day, attend a ribbon-cutting ceremony, promote the event on TV, and conduct workshops for people who came to the grand opening.

I initially declined the offer because it didn't involve me dancing. *What do I know about conducting a workshop?* I thought. *I'm a ballroom dancer.* But later, when I discussed the opportunity with Rick, he encouraged me to reconsider the invitation. It would give me a chance, he said, to share my story with others.

After giving it more thought, I realized that this would be yet another new life challenge. *I've got to do something I don't think I can do*, I decided. And I'm so glad I did.

Michael connected me with an exceptional talent agent, TinaMarie Holland, who helped me by taking care of all the details. And since Rick had given many speeches and conducted hundreds of workshops for his job, he helped me create a speech for the opening ceremony. I spent the next few weeks memorizing what I was going to say. We also planned an agenda for a one-hour workshop, which I would have to deliver three times throughout the day.

The company flew Rick and me out to Salt Lake City. TinaMarie and her husband, Garrett Steele—a country music recording artist and nationally ranked Pro-Angler—met us at the airport. For the next two days, they guided us around to the events. I was so grateful for their advice and professional wisdom.

The night before the grand opening, I was reviewing my speech for the ribbon-cutting ceremony and notes about what I would do in the workshops.

"Honey, I'm not going to use this," I said to Rick. "I need to go out there and just be myself."

"Are you sure?" he asked skeptically.

Rick is always super-prepared for anything like this. He couldn't believe that I was going to do this with no notes.

"Yes, I don't want to read my speech. I just want to be who I am."

The next morning, TinaMarie and Garrett picked us up and took us to the opening ceremony. When we arrived before the event, a TV station was in the new facility, filming a local news show hosted by two former Olympic athletes. There were about a dozen people in the room, and they wanted me to teach everyone a few ballroom dance steps. With the music blaring, we all danced as the host invited everyone watching to come out and attend my workshops.

The ribbon-cutting ceremony was attended by

several company executives and the mayor, as well as team members who worked in the new facility. I was introduced, and as I went to the podium, there was enthusiastic applause from the crowd. I thanked the company for inviting me and complimented them on the beautiful new facility. I also told them about my *AGT* story.

Then it was on to the first workshop. The room was packed, and my plan was to be natural and have a conversation with the group. I shared my dancing story and then opened it up for questions. For the next hour, I talked about everything from my diet to my exercise routine and demonstrated some of my dance moves. Since I juice vegetables, the company provided a juicer, and I showed them what I use in my "secret recipe" to stay fit and youthful. The time flew by, and before I knew it, it was time to do the next workshop. Some people stayed for all three sessions.

Afterward, as TinaMarie and Garrett were driving us to the airport, I felt so thankful that I had taken on this new, very different and fulfilling experience. Had I not acted on my instinct to do something I didn't think I could do, I would have missed an amazing opportunity.

Misha and I were also invited to appear at the ten-year anniversary of the Starz Ballroom Dance studio in Cleveland, Ohio. Liz Rice, owner of the studio, had been working as a manager on Lukasz's Arthur Murray studio team when I first started dancing. We became friends when I learned that she had been a star tennis player at the University of Florida. Liz has been a leader in the ballroom dance industry for many years and has a vibrant business in Cleveland. Misha and I accepted her invitation and had an amazing time. On the evening of the celebration, we danced two of our *AGT* routines. Liz's students were so excited we were there, and we spent hours answering their questions.

The next day, Liz gave us a tour of Cleveland, and we visited the Rock & Roll Hall of Fame and Museum. As we were leaving, fans at the Cleveland Browns football stadium next door were filing out after the game. Since Liz's car was parked on the other side of the stadium, she guided us quickly through the crowd. Suddenly, I heard screaming, "It's them! it's Quin and Misha from *America's Got Talent!*" A huge group quickly surrounded us, congratulating us and taking selfies. What surprised me was how many young kids knew about us. Liz commented, "I love hanging around you two, because we always get so much attention!" I remembered what the *AGT* executive had said to us: "*If you move on to the Live Show, your life will change forever.*" How right he was.

Although Misha and I had received many invitations to perform overseas in Thailand, China, and El Salvador, the timing had never worked out for us to accept. But Michael Chapman, Misha, and I decided that we would create a spectacular routine to perform at the prestigious Ohio Star Ball Anniversary Show in November 2018 in Columbus, Ohio— one of the oldest and largest ballroom dance competitions in the world. Michael was the executive producer of the show, and it took place in the massive Regency Ballroom that seats six thousand.. Our song selection was "Forever Young," sung by Louisa Johnson, and Michael choreographed a sensuous Bolero routine for us, full of ballroom dancing mixed with dangerous lifts and high-speed spins. There were large screens at one end of the ballroom, and as our performance began, scenes from our *AGT* performances flashed in the background.

It was magical dancing with Misha that night, as we glided to the emotional music. Our performance ended with a sustained standing ovation. As we left the dance floor, I noticed many people had been moved to tears. It was the perfect ending to an unforgettable year.

CHAPTER 20
GOING HOME

During my *AGT* experience, I received an outpouring of support in Thailand and many requests for interviews. Because of our non-stop schedule, I was not able to respond promptly to them, but now that I had more time, Rick and I made plans to travel to Thailand in December and January.

When we arrived at Bangkok's Suvarnabhumi Airport, I was surprised that several people recognized me and came up to greet me. They said they were so proud of me and knew I was Thai when they saw me give the *wai* at the end of the Golden Buzzer performance. We had this experience many times throughout the trip, and each time I was shocked. It seemed like I had become a celebrity to the people of Thailand.

It had been four years since our last visit, and I was so eager to be with my family again. The day after we arrived, we took a one-hour flight to Khon Kaen, where my family, including all my sisters and brothers, were there to greet us with overwhelming emotion. We then drove about forty minutes from the airport to our home in the village. One of my nieces served as my public relations assistant and made all our arrangements to attend a variety of ceremonies. In my village, we were welcomed by a parade with people dancing in the streets to traditional Thai music. We visited the village school and the Wat. There was also a special ceremony at the hospital in Chiang Yuen, the small town closest to

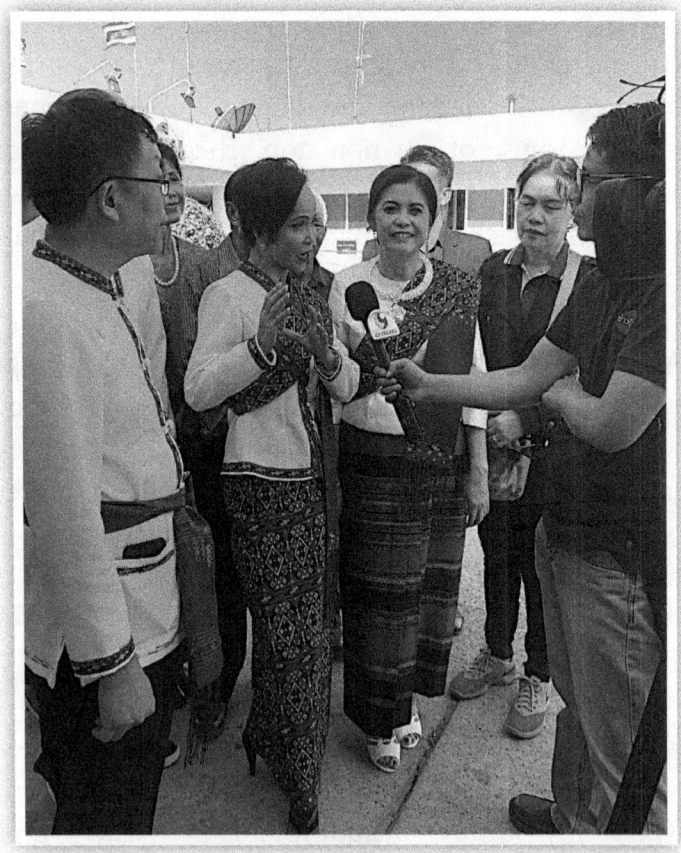

GOING HOME

our village. The hospital officials organized an incredible event that included traditional Thai dancers in elaborate costumes. They had also arranged for special costumes to be made for Rick and me. I was invited to join the Thai dancing while the television cameras rolled. Afterwards, I was interviewed by the local TV news station, and the segment was aired throughout the country.

During our visit, we also spent a month crisscrossing Thailand and sharing my story with the beautiful people of my homeland.

We also met with Mr. Sutichai Yoon, who had contacted me immediately after the *AGT* Golden Buzzer performance. When I asked my niece about him, she gasped, "Auntie, he is a very famous man! He has his own TV show!" I asked her to contact Mr. Sutichai, and he said he wanted to do an interview "to light up Thailand!" I learned that he was the primary anchor for the Thai PBS news show; former CEO of Nation Multimedia Group, one of Thailand's largest media companies; and one of the foremost media moguls in the country. Many people referred to him as the "Larry King of Thailand."

My interview with Mr. Sutichai was scheduled for January 5, 2019. He wanted to do it outside, so we arranged to conduct it in the backyard of my niece's house. He arrived with his film crew for the one-hour interview. As it progressed, Mr. Sutichai learned more about my story and that I came from the village. He became fascinated, and the interview continued for several more hours. At the end of our session, he told me his own story about his meager village upbringing, and we established an instant bond.

Our interview turned into a four-segment series that aired on national TV the next week, on four consecutive nights in prime time. It was surreal being at our home in the village, crowded around a small TV with my sisters and brothers, watching myself

GOING HOME

being interviewed. My family was so proud that their sister had become famous. As we watched, my mind flashed back six decades to the little girl who desperately wanted to leave the village and "be somebody—to be seen."

I closed my eyes and in prayer said, *Thank you, God! All the glory goes to You!*

CHAPTER 21

BOLD CHALLENGES

After returning home in January, I knew that it was time to slow down and make decisions about what to do next with my life. My schedule had been nonstop since *AGT*, and I never had the opportunity to savor and reflect on this amazing, once-in-a-lifetime experience.

The first step was to move out of the apartment in Jacksonville that we had rented while training for *AGT*. Misha helped Rick load the furniture onto a U-Haul truck, and as Rick drove off, Misha and I went to our favorite Thai restaurant for lunch. We reminisced about the incredible times we had together during the past six years, and I told Misha that there were many things I still wanted to do. The most important was to begin writing my book. I also wanted to learn to dance International Latin. However, because writing my story was such a time-consuming process, there was no way that I could continue driving five hours a day, as I had before. We thought about the idea of sharing the commute, so that I would drive one week and Misha would drive the next. In the end, though, we both decided that it would be better for me to hold off, so that I would have the time I needed for the book and Misha could continue teaching his students in Jacksonville.

Two years before Misha and I went on *AGT*, I saw that a new Fred Astaire dance studio had opened close to my house. One day soon after, on my way home after working out for a couple of hours at the gym, I dropped by the studio to say hello. The owners were a married couple, Hayk Balasanyan and Emilia Poghosyan. I had never met them or heard about them, but later learned that they were the U.S. International Latin champions. When I went into the studio, I felt a sense of warmth and love from both of them right away. I told them that I was interested in learning International Latin, and when they asked me if I had danced before, I simply said "a little bit."

Now, two years later, I decided to reconnect with them. Because of *AGT*, they now knew who I was, and they both made me feel so warm and special when I came into their studio again.

"You fooled me, Quin!" Emilia laughed. "When you first met us, you said you danced only 'a little bit.'" To this day, she loves to remind me of this.

I told them that I wanted to learn to dance Inter-

BOLD CHALLENGES

national Latin, but not compete.

"Why do you want to learn International Latin? It's hard!" Hayk said, surprised.

"That's exactly why I want to learn it," I said with conviction.

"Okay, let's do it!" he said.

The timing was perfect for me. I could write my book *and* learn International Latin, since their studio was only five minutes from my house. I believe that God opened this amazing opportunity for me.

I had heard from some coaches that it would take at least two years to learn this difficult style. For the next few months, Hayk taught me Latin from the beginning, and I made rapid progress. Hayk is a warm and loving spirit who teaches with passion. When you first meet him, you fall in love with his genuine humbleness, his big heart, his lively sense of humor, and his talent. There is never a dull moment with Hayk, and we always laughed so hard in every session. His coaching was exactly what I needed.

Because it was time-consuming to write the book, I would go in for a lesson only twice a week. Afterward, I would practice alone, every opportunity I could. I really surprised myself that I was learning so fast. I believe that when you find your purpose, you find your passion. And when you find your passion, that's when you find your power.

Because of my rapid progress, Hayk put a routine together so we could accelerate our practice. After six months, I told him that I wanted to try to compete

FEARLESS GIRL

again. It had been over two years since I last competed, and the United States Dance Championships was coming up in a couple of months.

"You want to dance at USDC?" Hayk asked incredulously.

"Yes," I said. "I just want to see how I feel being back on the dance floor again."

So in September 2019, we were on the USDC dancefloor, competing against the best senior Latin dancers who, in some instances, had been dancing for decades. After only six months of total International Latin experience, we astonishingly finished in second place in my age group in the Open Gold Scholarship, which was unheard of. I am so grateful to Hayk and Emilia for giving me the training, the

BOLD CHALLENGES

support, and the opportunity.

The Theater Arts style of dancing also attracted me. On *AGT*, Misha and I were using this style, even though we never competed in it. With its lifts, spins, and dips, it is like dancing and acrobatics combined. To me it is roller-coaster-level excitement, while Rick refers to it as "dangerous dancing."

Michael suggested that I consider doing Theater Arts with Craig Smith in a show. Craig is a many-times World and British Theater Arts champion and coach who previously worked with us when we were on *AGT*, helping Misha with lifts. He was excited about the idea, and we mapped out a plan for me to begin learning this style. With Michael as our coach and choreographer, he and Craig crafted a spectacular theatrical production, which we would perform at the prestigious Ohio Star Ball show coming up in November.

Craig is a perfectionist and a brilliant teacher. He is patient and very detailed in his instruction. He explains things in a way that is very easy to understand way and makes sure that I'm clear about everything before I am lifted or thrown into the air. During each practice, he is fully engaged and focused, and he raised my commitment to the highest level. Because of the extreme nature of this type of training, we would meet only twice a week. During some sessions, he would have his professional partner, Andrea Harvey, teach me the finer points from the partner's perspective, and her coaching was extremely helpful.

For the next several months, Craig and I worked tirelessly with two other amazing dancers who were in the show—David Scott and Maiky Ayala from Hardrive Productions in Orlando. The show's Asian theme told the story of a princess who is pursued by three admirers. A fight results, and Craig emerges as the victor. The heart of the dance expresses our love story. The stirring music was blended from two movies—the songs "A Love Before Time" from *Crouching Tiger, Hidden Dragon* and "Red Warrior" from *The Last Samurai*.

In November 2019, performing in front of a standing-room-only audience of more than six thousand, in a show that was aired on pay-per-view TV, we made our grand entrance. I was carried in doing the splits over David and Maiky's shoulders, as the master of ceremony introduced us:

This remarkable lady is a wife, a mother, a grandmother, a mentor, and Pro-Am ballroom champion.

Quin, at seventy-two, defies gravity and all expectations.

With over 32 million YouTube viewers, she has inspired all of us with her heart.

She says, "I don't live to dance; I dance to live!

Age doesn't define you; you do.

When you have a dream, run after it, and take bold risks.

Love, respect, kindness, and compassion can change your life."

BOLD CHALLENGES

Tonight's performance is a tribute to her homeland.

Please welcome Quin, with Craig, David and Maiky.

The live performance went even better than our many rehearsals. In our final bows to the audience, we left the dance floor to rousing applause. I was blessed and honored to have danced with the master of Theater Arts, and I am very grateful to both Craig and Hayk for the incredible experiences they gave me. My life continued to amaze me.

And then, unexpectedly, I had the most severe health challenge that I have ever faced as an adult. Shingles attacked my eye, face, and head. It is a very scary disease that can cause blindness if it's not treated quickly. My family physician, Dr. Pursley, immediately put me in contact with an ophthalmologist, who saw me right away. My doctors did all they could to help me through this condition, but there is no cure. The medication, especially the pain pills, left me feeling limp and weak. I had no energy and could barely speak. I prayed to God continuously for relief. After suffering for many weeks, I decided to quit taking the pain pills because of the severe side effects. The pain continued, but at least I didn't feel sedated all the time.

It has been a long, hard journey to get back to where I was before this virus hit me. The aftereffects of shingles are still with me today, including severe itching and eye discomfort. I lost a lot of hair on the right side of my head because of blisters and nerve damage, and the doctors have no idea when, or even if, the illness will clear up completely. I had to stop working on my book for over a year. But at least I didn't go blind. My faith is stronger than my fear, and I refuse to let this discomfort get in the way of what I need to do—but I strongly recommend that everyone get the shingles vaccine.

Then, finally, just as I started getting my energy back and working out again, the COVID-19 pandemic hit. As we all know, normal life stopped for the world. No dancing, no gym, and no competing. I used this time to continue rebuilding my health and fitness. Although gyms and dance studios were closed, Rick

BOLD CHALLENGES

and I found a trail near our home and would run, stretch, and jump. I also expanded my vegetable and fruit garden in the backyard, so we can eat healthy organic food every day.

At last, when COVID vaccines were rolled out in 2021, I started training again with both Craig and Hayk. I set a goal of competing in the United Stated Dance Championships in both International Latin

and Theater Arts styles that September. I challenged myself to become better and better in each dance. Meanwhile, for the Millennium Dancesport Competition in June, Michael and Craig created a new performance around Beyonce's song "Listen." As the chorography was shaped, it became a highly emotional storyline. The song was featured in the film *Dreamgirls,* and its lyrics refer to tenacity, love, the refusal to defer dreams, and reaching for fame. Rick was captivated by this production, especially since he has taught Listening at the college level for over three decades. Michael invited him to craft introductory words for the three-minute routine, which contained multiple dangerous lifts and spins, threaded between dance steps. When we performed "Listen" for the first time and took our final pose to rousing applause, we both felt a huge rush of accomplishment and excitement.

Hayk and I also competed in the International Latin Senior 2 Open Gold division, and we won this event, which was totally unexpected.

When things are going good, work harder.

Finally, on September 9, 2021, I competed in the United States Dance Championships in both styles. It was an unimaginable day for me. First, Hayk and I won the National Senior 2 International Latin Championship. Then, after just a few hours' break, Craig and I performed "Listen" in the Theater Arts event and won the National Championship, against competitors who were seventeen years old and up.

BOLD CHALLENGES

Winning two national championships on the same day, at the age of seventy-three, was beyond imagining. I am so grateful to Hayk and Craig for their dedication to helping me become my very best self, after two years of painful challenges.

CHAPTER 22
SACRIFICE

People ask me all the time, "How do you do it? How are you so fit? So strong? So brave?" I have many answers, of course. It's not one single thing—there's no magic pill that got me where I am today. Through the years, I've given simple, honest responses: *Work hard. Don't give up. Follow your passion.* Some people hear these words, but they don't absorb them. Most people, I think, want quick and easy answers, and few are willing to do the hard work it takes to achieve results.

In hindsight, I have come to realize that one of my secrets—how I have managed to stay fit and forever youthful even into my seventh decade of living—is *sacrifice*. Most people don't really like to sacrifice. They prefer the idea of *compromise*—giving up a little bit rather than a lot.

But sacrifice is fundamental to achieving greatness. Compromise leads to incremental progress, whereas sacrifice will have you leaping across chasms. Before I turned sixty, I compromised and felt the effects. When I was playing tennis, for example, I wondered why I would get tired. It was all because of my diet. In those day, I would "live to eat" rather than "eat to live," which is what I do now.

Today, I think back to the hundreds of dinners I missed with friends, dozens of trips not taken with Rick, and countless mornings not spent snuggling under warm covers. Instead, I have chosen to eat every meal with intention. I am aware of my body in ways that others might not understand. When I have a cookie, for instance, I can practically feel the sugar rushing through my body, and, if I eat two cookies, I will likely be bloated the next day. For some people, that's okay. For me, it is not. I eat fruits and vegetables from plants that I care for in my backyard garden. I have chosen to live the healthiest possible life I can, from sunup to sundown. I eat exactly the right food

SACRIFICE

for me—for the lifestyle I want to sustain—every day. No cheat days. No days off. Almost no sugar. I have built a life around staying fit and young. My body is sacred, and I listen to it reverently.

If you want something, you must give up something. We cannot have it all and still be great. Because I've yearned to be *somebody* since my days as a poor young girl, my target has always been greatness. *Good enough* is never enough. Mediocrity, for me, is a crime. I have always needed to stand out, not blend in. My target has always been excellence—a life that is extraordinary and filled with achievements.

To realize that dream, I have sacrificed. I lost friends that I had for more than forty years—dear, kind people who could not understand my unyielding focus and thirst for perfection. Once I achieved a level of greatness—especially after the Golden Buzzer on *AGT*—I was unprepared for the fact that many people I had known for decades suddenly didn't seem to know how to talk to me. There was awkwardness and an invisible wall between us. The harder I worked to become an extraordinary dancer, and the more I worked to achieve excellence, the lonelier my life became. I have accepted this truth: *Achievements will create distance. And differences become disconnections.* And I came to embrace loneliness as a constant companion.

To win, one must live with a singular focus. Every choice I make, from the time I wake up until the time I close my eyes, is intentional. My ability to dance like I'm in my twenties is the result of hundreds of thousands of sacrifices I've made and continue to make every day, with no plans to stop. My age is just a number. I do not feel like I'm in my mid-seventies. In fact, I am fitter and healthier today than I was in my thirties and forties. I understand that everything I put into my body is either one step toward my goal or one step away from it. Every food produces a consequence—a result that makes the target more or less achievable.

I sacrifice the expected seventy-five-year-old-way-of-life so that I can stay active, God willing, for many years to come—and so that my days aren't spent in doctors' offices. Many people my age (and younger) are taking many prescription medications. They're ingesting dozens of pills every day, and they deal with the side effects of those medications. They endure varying levels of immobility. They suffer from aches, pains, and constant tiredness. But I am free from medication; I get up at 4:30 am every day, and I read and study before sunrise to start my day.

I understand that this life makes me different and strange to people. But I am also willing to sacrifice being understood, even accepted, so that I can feel healthy. My friends and family have struggled to understand this. I do, however, willingly give up my routine to spend quality time with them.

Sacrifice has become an important part of *my way*. Just like in tennis, I hate to lose more than love to win.

CHAPTER 23
HUMBLE AND HUNGRY

I don't discuss my feelings of pride very often. I share my wisdom with people because I've been asked to, repeatedly, by folks young and old—those who have watched me in the ballroom and those who found me on *America's Got Talent*. People usually want to know my secrets, but they rarely ask me how I feel.

And if they did? I'd say that I feel both humble and hungry. That I hate to lose more than I love to win. If someone asked me with genuine curiosity how I felt, I'd tell them that I feel accomplished but unfinished. That I'm still "on call" and have no plans to settle down.

If I do feel proud, I don't hold onto that feeling for long. I smile, briefly. I recognize my ability to do something great—after lots of hard work. I know the sensations that come from achieving success against all odds. Of surprising people. Sometimes of surprising myself! I feel the resolve coursing through my veins—it's what propelled me to drive five hours a day to and from dance practice, four days a week for five years, just to inch a step closer to achieving my dream. I am proud I survived my childhood. That I married Rick. That I learned to speak English and became a mother and grandmother!

HUMBLE AND HUNGRY

I am proud, but only fleetingly. There is an urgency that propels me to move forward. To do more. To achieve at a higher level. I am hungry for it. I'm not ready to settle in yet, to cozy up on a couch with a blanket around my legs and reminisce about a life well lived. I'm still living it! *If I get comfortable, I'm done,* I think to myself. *When things are going good, work harder!* I have always lived by this mantra. I need the momentum—knowing that the more I win, the more I'll win, which is really a universal truth.

I work for success. I train for hours and hours every day. I stretch. I lift weights. I run. I eat for nourishment, not pleasure. I dance. I make decisions based on what I want, always focusing on the target. I don't need the attention and I don't want to be distracted. Whether my target is close or far away, I behave as if I'm a sniper, with my goal in the crosshairs.

I don't sleep more than four hours these days. My mind travels. At 2:00 am, sometimes I think, *Maybe you shouldn't be spending time working so hard. What if the reward isn't there this time? Isn't it feeling a little much?* But by the time the sun comes up, everything looks different. And like the sun, I rise. I seek out exertion. I go to the gym. I run on the treadmill. I lift weights. I stretch for an hour. There's no stopping. I am insatiable. Forward movement. Onward. I know that if I stop now, I'll be at the finish line.

Nowadays, I am more grateful than I am anything else. My experiences keep me humble. Yesterday is

FEARLESS GIRL

past tense. Good or bad, it's over. Now I live for today and for tomorrow. I wake up every morning, humble and hungry, to the smell of new opportunity. I am Quin, and I don't have to be more than who I am, and who I can be.

CONCLUSION

I turned seventy-five a few months ago. There was no big party, only a small gathering of family members—just the way I like it. I've got bigger plans—not for a party, but for celebrating each day of life that God blesses me with, going forward full speed!

I feel like I'm able to write my own rules about what age means. I've come to realize I have never acted my age. I lost my childhood to poverty, hunger, and illness; I worked on the farm with my sisters and brothers, when most American kids were still playing with dolls and marbles, and I never stopped working for almost two decades.

I am so grateful to have beaten the odds. I survived an adolescence that others did not; I escaped from poverty.

I met and fell in love with an American soldier who then sent for me to come to America on a fiancé visa. And that was a rare thing indeed. And I've been married to Rick, my soulmate—fifty happy years later. Without Rick, I wouldn't be Quin. I would still be Kim. I am soever grateful to him. I am most grateful to God's miracle for uniting us together from complete opposite sides of the world.

Becoming a tennis champ in my thirties, learning ballroom dance and becoming a World and United States champion in my sixties and a Golden Buzzer winner at age seventy-one? How could this all happen?

CONCLUSION

I know it's not just by luck. I love a challenge, and for me, all of life is a challenge! My plans are big! I want to try out again for *America's Got Talent* when I'm eighty. And in the meantime? I'll keep training harder than ever—learning, growing, and dancing. And this year, special things are happening.

I was approached by a film company in California, Silver Screen Studios, to be part of a documentary film honoring seniors who are doing amazing work in the senior community. In April 2022, the film crew came to Orlando and interviewed me and Hayk and filmed us dancing.

When the producer asked Hayk, "How would you describe Quin?" he responded in his humorous, direct way, "Quin is like an alien bird! She gives 150 percent effort in every lesson and flies higher and higher."

The film premiered in Orlando in September 2022. And I am very excited to share that Misha and I have reunited and will soon be performing a new version of "Forever Young."

The road ahead may or may not be paved with golden confetti—only time will tell. But I don't intend to stop. I am not afraid of getting older. I'm not afraid to try new things and fail. After all, I've done it all my life. I can't stop now!

And I leave you with this thought:

All of our lives have many ups and downs.

But when things are going good, work harder.

FEARLESS GIRL

Dream it! Believe it! Be it!
Love, Quin

ACKNOWLEDGEMENTS

I extend my deepest and heartfelt gratitude to the many people who have helped me bring *Fearless Girl* to life. It has taken more than three years to write my story and more than seven decades to live it.

First, I am so blessed and eternally grateful for my husband and soulmate, Rick. Without him, my story would have ended in Thailand. He has been my everything, and I love him forever.

I am indebted to the team of writers that worked tirelessly to write my story as I shared it with them including Lori Coffae, Jenna Glatzer, and Rick. Their incomparable talent and creativity have captured the true spirit of my life. I am grateful to Susan Wels who contributed her editing expertise and Jay Monroe for his extraordinary design talent in bringing the book to its final form.

I am so thankful to my family in America, including my son, Mark and my grandchildren, Emily, Mark Jr., and Casey. I am especially grateful for all my family members in Thailand. My two "adopted" sisters, Truly Higgins and Tiew Honig, have supported me in every way, especially with my dancing and throughout the *AGT* journey. I am blessed by my "god daughter" Rose Rosae.

I owe great thanks to Doragnes Bradshaw for her dedicated leadership with my social media. I also appreciate the time and energy that Jan Crisostomo spent helping Misha and me on Twitter during *AGT*, and my "adopted" niece, Loni Higgins Gregory, was my special cheerleader on social media throughout my *AGT* experience.

There have been many special and loving spirits who have been involved with my dance journey, including my dance partners Romney Reyes, Misha Vlasov, Hayk Balasanyan, and Craig Smith and my dance coaches, Lukasz Rogowski, Michael Chapman, Emilia Poghosyan, and Marina & Vasily Vlasov.

I extend my deepest appreciation to the media leaders who took an interest in me, including *Growing Bolder* Executive Vice President Bill Shafer and CEO Marc Middleton and Thai media executive and television personality Mr. Sutichai Yoon.

I am also grateful for the warm hospitality extended to me at the Royal Thai Consulate in Los Angeles and the kindness of Thai Consul General Mr. Tanee Sangrat and Lieutenant Consul Gunpirom Vichathorn. And I especially appreciated the tremendous outpouring of support from the Thailand Foundation and so many people in Thailand.

I am deeply thankful to the *America's Got Talent* team, including celebrity judges Simon Cowell, Heidi

ACKNOWLEDGEMENTS

Klum, Mel B, and Howie Mandel, and owe a special thank you to judge Martina McBride, who gave us the Golden Buzzer; to Master of Ceremonies Tyra Banks; and to the executive producers and producers, especially Alexa Keane and Liza Pablico; the film crews and interviewers; all of the contestants; and the audiences who were so welcoming and enthusiastic.

I am especially grateful for the love and support of: Wini and Frank Hagy, Shari Oxman, Andrea Harvey, Liz Rice, Mary Murphy, Tony Tang, Larry Dean, Pamela Bolling, Eddie Rivera, Carol Ann Duncan, Linda Gill, Lisa Lowery, Shelia Smith Davis, Maria McGill and Sommer Gray, Renae and Tony Sterling, Denise and Dr. William Neman, Dr. Dmitriy Model, Laura and Bob Cornett, Penn Lincoln, and Paul Thesasiri.

Most importantly, all the glory goes to God, who has directed my steps on the incredible path my life has taken.

QUIN POROS BOMMELJE
Performance | Motivation | Inspiration

WHAT CAN QUIN DO FOR YOU?
PERFORMANCES, MOTIVATIONAL SPEAKING, TV, RADIO, & PUBLIC APPEARANCES.

Defying gravity, this remarkable mother, wife, grandmother, mentor and dancer has inspired so many with her talent and mental strength.

She is paving the way for women of all ages. Strength, age and ability are what you define them to be. When you find your purpose, you find your passion. And when you find you passion, you unleash your power.

Her every-day mantra is *"When things are going good.....Work Harder!"*

"Dream It! Believe It! Be It!"

Please visit: QUININSPIRE.COM
email: QUIN@QUININSPIRE.COM

ABOUT THE AUTHOR

Quin Poros Bommelje grew up in poverty in a small village in northeast Thailand, struggling to survive until she left home to find work in the nearby city in her teenage years. For several years, she worked and lived at a small restaurant, then eventually started work at an American air base during the Vietnam War. There, she met her future husband, Rick.

Her first-ever airplane flight was to Orlando, Florida, to marry Rick. She took classes at a community college and worked as a waitress while he also attended college, and they had a son. Quin and her son both found a love of tennis, and she played competitively for thirty years, ranking fifth in Florida in her age group. When a pre-skin cancer scare put an end to her tennis career, she found a new passion in dance.

Although she didn't set foot in a dance studio until age sixty, she quickly climbed the ranks and is now a World and National Senior American Rhythm dance champion many times over. She and her partner, Misha Vlasov, entered the thirteenth season of *America's Got Talent* and received a Golden Buzzer from guest judge Martina McBride in the Judge's Cut round. More than 32 million have viewed this performance on YouTube. Quin and Misha advanced to the Live Show and performed at the Dolby Theater in front of 18 million viewers.

Today, Quin continues to excel on the dance floor. She is the 2021 United States Theater Arts champion and the United States Senior International Latin champion. Her message is about the lifelong journey to stay fit and forever young.

—Quin Bommelje
email: quin@quinspire.com
Facebook: quininspire page
Instagram: quininspire

ABOUT THE AUTHOR

TELEVISION APPEARANCES

Sutichai Live (Thailand) Prime Time TV
Jan. 8-11, 2019

Americas Got Talent Season 13 NBC Quarterfinals
August 21, 2018

Americas Got Talent Season 13 NBC Judge's Cut Round
July 31, 2018

Americas Got Talent Season 13 NBC Celebrity Judges
July 2, 2018

MAJOR DANCE COMPETITIONS

World Championship, Winner Senior Open Rhythm, August 2016 Irvine, CA

World Championship, Winner Senior Open Rhythm, August 2015 Irvine, CA

World Championship, Vice Champion Ladies C Open Rhythm, August 2015 Irvine, CA

World Championship, Winner Senior Open Rhythm, August 2014 Irvine, CA

World Championship, Winner S1 Open Rhythm, August 2010 Columbus, OH

FEARLESS GIRL

United States Dance Championships, Winner, Pro/Am Theater Arts, September 2021, Orlando, FL

United States Dance Championships, Winner, Senior 2 International Latin, September 2021, Orlando, FL

United States Dance Championship, Winner S1 Open Rhythm, September 2017, Orlando, FL

United States Dance Championship, Winner Rising Star Open Rhythm, September 2015, Orlando, FL

United States Dance Championship, Vice Champion Ladies 'B' Open Rhythm, September 2014, Orlando, FL

United States Dance Championship, Vice Champion Ladies 'B' Open Rhythm, September 2011, Orlando, FL

United States Dance Championship, Vice Champion Ladies 'B' Open Rhythm, September 2009, Orlando, FL

Ohio Star Ball, Winner Senior Open Rhythm, November 2017, Columbus, OH

Ohio Star Ball, Vice Champion Ladies C Open Rhythm, November 2017, Columbus, OH

Ohio Star Ball, Winner Senior Open Rhythm, November 2016, Columbus, OH

ABOUT THE AUTHOR

Ohio Star Ball, Winner Senior Open Rhythm, November 2015, Columbus, OH

Ohio Star Ball, Winner Senior Open Rhythm, November 2014, Columbus, OH

Millennium Dancesport, Winner Senior 2 International Latin Open, June 2021, Orlando, FL

Millennium Dancesport, Winner Senior Open Rhythm, June 2017, Orlando, FL

Millennium Dancesport, Winner Senior Open Rhythm, June 2016, Orlando, FL

Millennium Dancesport, Winner Senior Open Rhythm, June 2015, Orlando, FL

Millennium Dancesport, Winner Senior Open Rhythm, June 2014, Orlando, FL

Millennium Dancesport, Winner Senior Open Rhythm, June 2013, Orlando, FL

Millennium Dancesport, Winner Senior Open Rhythm, June 2012, Orlando, FL

Hollywood Dancesport, Winner Ladies "C" Open Rhythm, November 2011, Los Angeles, CA

Emerald Ball Dancesport Championships, Winner Ladies Senior 1 Open Rhythm, April 2017, Los Angeles, CA

FEARLESS GIRL

Emerald Ball Dancesport Championships, Vice Champion Ladies "C" Open Rhythm, April 2017, Los Angeles, CA

Fred Astaire National Championship, Winner, Senior International Latin, November 2021, Orlando, FL

Arthur Murray Superama, Winner Open Rhythm 'B', October 2009, Las Vegas, NV

Arthur Murray Superama, Winner Open Smooth 'B', October 2009, Las Vegas, NV

SPECIAL DANCE PERFORMANCES

Ohio Star Ball, Anniversary Show, Columbus, OH, November 2020

Ohio Star Ball, Anniversary Show, Columbus, OH, November 2018

St. Johns County Dancing with the Stars,
St. Augustine, FL
July 2018

Millennium Dancesport Performance,
New Orleans, LA
June 2018

ABOUT THE AUTHOR

Growing Bolder Award Ceremony, Orlando, FL
January 2018

Ohio Star Ball, 40th Anniversary Show,
Columbus, OH,
November 2017

Dance Legends, New York, NY
April 2016

Dance, Dream & Inspire, Hard Rock Live,
Orlando, FL
September 2013

DOCUMENTARY FILM

Devoted Silver Screen Film Series: 2022

INTERVIEWS

Daily Mail: August 2018

Access Hollywood Live: August 2018

USA Today: August 2018

Thai BBC Service: August 2018

AARP: August 2018

FEARLESS GIRL

Good Housekeeping: August 2018

The St. Augustine Record: August 2018

Growing Bolder: May 2011

TENNIS

Played for thirty years

Ranked #5 in Florida in Women's 35 Age Group

Coached Girls Tennis Team, Lake Highland Preparatory School, Orlando, FL

Taught club tennis lessons for 10 years

www.ingramcontent.com/pod-product-compliance
Lightning Source LLC
Chambersburg PA
CBHW071311110426
42743CB00042B/1258